THE YOUNG TURKS

Prelude to the Revolution of 1908

THE YOUNG TURKS

Prelude to the Revolution
of 1908

BY ERNEST EDMONDSON RAMSAUR, JR.

NEW YORK / RUSSELL & RUSSELL

To my wife

and to the memory of my brother

Foreword

BY L. V. THOMAS

WHAT WAS happening in Turkey during the first decade of the present century has proved to be of direct importance not only for the late Ottomans and their successors of the Turkish Republic. The events leading up to the Young Turkish Revolutions and the Young Turk period also had their consequences in the Balkans, among the Arabs, and for peoples still more distant from Istanbul. Yet this entire subject, which Dr. Ramsaur here studies up to the Revolution of 1908, has as yet received relatively scant attention in English.

This book, moreover, will also deserve the attention of readers whose interest is in the more general, but certainly pressing, problems of how the ideas of western nationalism entered and established themselves in non-western parts of the world, of how those ideas embodied themselves there in new political institutions, and of how individual leaders in such regions are contriving, with greater or less success, to best the local oppositions to their efforts and to assert themselves and their "causes" on their local scenes and in their international relations.

Nowhere in Asia or Africa where today a local, nationalist "liberation" or "anti-colonial" movement is active, does that movement lack leaders who themselves either have studied and lived in the west, as did most of the men whom Dr. Ramsaur introduces, or at the least have come under strong western influence. To point this out is not, of course, to argue that in any single instance history has repeated itself, or is likely to. It is simply to assert again that knowledge of what has happened is a precious key to understanding of what is happening. For that reason, this book is both welcome and timely.

L. V. THOMAS

Princeton University
September 4, 1956

vii

Preface

THIS BOOK has been written over a long period of time and in a great many places since it was begun as a doctoral dissertation. It has suffered interruptions from a number of causes, including war, but it has also benefited to some extent from the author's wanderings. A tour as American Vice Consul in Istanbul from 1948 to 1950, for example, afforded the author another opportunity to talk with some of the participants in the revolution of 1908.

The result of this work of many years and many interruptions is still far from perfect, but the author has at length concluded that he is never likely to have the opportunity to repair all the imperfections. The book does, it is felt, fill a certain gap. Critics, especially Turkish critics, will undoubtedly find a number of errors, both of omission and commission, but it is the author's conviction that the findings in general will bear scrutiny.

Some of the author's Turkish friends will undoubtedly disagree with certain interpretations and analyses, particularly where personalities are concerned. It is sincerely hoped that they will realize that the opinions were honestly arrived at and that they are as disinterested as it is humanly possible for them to be. No one, it is hoped, will question the author's esteem for Turkey and the Turks.

No one can undertake such a work as this without becoming deeply indebted to a number of persons. The author's greatest single debt is to the late Professor Robert J. Kerner of the University of California who suggested the subject and under whose direction the work was begun in 1939. The debt to Professor Kerner is far larger than this would indicate in itself, however, for the author learned from Professor Kerner as much as he could absorb in many other fields.

Professor William L. Langer of Harvard University was stimulating, encouraging, and extremely helpful while the author was working at the Widener Library in 1940-1941.

One of the greatest debts of all is owed to the late Dr. John

Kingsley Birge of Istanbul. Dr. Birge collected materials and forwarded them to the author in the early days of the war—materials which now would be unavailable. In 1948 when the author returned to Turkey, he found Dr. Birge as much a source of help and inspiration as ever. With Dr. Birge's death in 1952, the world lost a great scholar and an admirable gentleman.

Several of the author's Turkish friends honored him by reading all or part of the manuscript in 1950. They include Halide Edip Adıvar, the late Dr. Adnan Adıvar, and Dr. Nihat Reşat Belger.

The late Riza Tevfik Bey wrote the author several letters which he will always treasure, and he is deeply grateful for the fact that he was able to meet and know Riza Tevfik Bey before his death in 1950.

Dr. Ernst Jaeckh, now of Columbia University, was most helpful in two meetings widely separated in space and time.

Professor Marshall Dill, Jr., now of Bard College, kindly made some notes of his available to the author.

Acknowledgment is also made to the University of California for a travelling fellowship and numerous teaching fellowships; to the American Council of Learned Societies for several kindnesses; and to the American Foreign Service for assigning the author to Istanbul from 1948 to 1950—even if they did not know how he proposed to spend some of his spare time.

While the debt to all those mentioned above—and to a great many others—is a very real one, full responsibility for what was done with their help rests on the author. That is to say, the conclusions drawn and the opinions expressed in this work all reflect the views of the author alone. In particular, attention is invited to the fact that the author's connection with the American Foreign Service does not imply that this book expresses the views of the Department of State.

E. E. Ramsaur, Jr.

A Note on Transliteration

FEW MODIFICATIONS for the American or English reader are necessary in rendering Turkish names. In this book the Turkish letters C, Ş, and Ç have been rendered as J, Sh, and Ch wherever they have occurred in the text. There is no equivalent for the undotted I (pronounced like the i in "bird").

Proper names have ordinarily been given as they occur in modern Turkish unless there is an accepted English variant. Thus Abdul Hamid is used throughout in place of modern Turkish Abdülhamit.

Contents

THE YOUNG TURKS

Prelude to the Revolution of 1908

CHAPTER I

Introduction—The Background

THE YOUNG TURK REVOLUTION OF 1908 was the culmination of many decades of activity by a small group of liberals or pseudo-liberals who had gradually, under the influence of western ideas and concepts, come to the conclusion that the Ottoman Empire was doomed to extinction if drastic steps were not taken to check the decay which had set in. The movement can be traced back to the reign of the profligate and sensuous Sultan Abdul Aziz (1861-1876), who allowed the reforms undertaken by his predecessor, Abdul Mejid (1839-1861), to remain a dead letter and had no interest in anything but the indulgence of his own fancies. During the reign of Abdul Aziz, however, the Ottoman Empire began to feel the impact of western civilization in ever-increasing volume, for with the Crimean War western Europe became more and more aware of the Eastern Question and its implications.

With the rapid spread of western ideas, the Turkish intelligentsia began to stir. Turkish literature, which had never been great in its own right, commenced to turn its back on the influences which had made it a stereotyped imitation of Persian literature and to welcome new influences which were to make it, for a time, at least, an almost lifeless imitation of French literature. In so doing, Turkish literary figures came into contact with a new and wholly different culture which stirred their imaginations and gave them much food for thought. Much of what they were now exposed to they could not understand, for there was nothing in their background to prepare them for it. Thus many of the ideas that they now began to express in Turkish were ill-digested, and even the vocabulary they used was not really assimilated. But the important thing was that they were beginning to use words like "fatherland," "constitution," and "parliament," all of which sounded very strange and out-of-place in the sprawling, moribund, multinational Ottoman Empire—so

3

much so that they soon found themselves forced to express their views from positions outside the empire.

Thus it was in the 1860's that the first Young Turks became a familiar sight on the boulevards of Paris and London. Around 1864 the first Young Turk journal, *Hurriet* (*Liberty*),[1] was founded in London under the editorship of Rifat Bey, and a colony of Young Turks was established. It included the leading exponents of the new trend in Turkish literature, Kemal Bey (Namık Kemal) and Ziya Pasha, and such others as Mustafa Fazıl Pasha, brother of Khedive Ismail of Egypt, Nuri Bey, Reshat Bey, and Ali Suavi. The last was later to lose his life in a vain attempt to rescue the deposed Sultan Murat V from the palace in which he was confined by Abdul Hamid.[2]

This early Young Turk movement, primarily literary in its inception, soon began to take on a political complexion. Under the influence of western European institutions and customs, its leaders began to demand freedom from the despotism of the Turkish Sultans and the adoption of constitutional government in the Ottoman Empire. There was a widespread impression that a strong modern state would automatically come into being if western European patterns were simply translated into the empire. Their thinking was beginning to betray signs of nationalism as well. Like later generations of Young Turks, they saw reform as a means of strengthening a dying empire rather than as an end in itself. By borrowing western institutions they hoped to gain strength to repulse the encroachments of the West.

Again like their successors, they were prepared to welcome the cooperation of the minorities of the empire. No more than the revolutionists of 1908 did they conceive of the minorities as equal partners, however. Their design was to strengthen the Ottoman Empire; implicit in this was the continuation of Turkish supremacy.

The political activity of the Young Turks of Abdul Aziz's

[1] Modern Turkish *Hürriyet*.
[2] See below, note 14.

4

day was confined largely to the publishing of newspapers which were sent into the empire by means of the foreign postoffices, which enjoyed extraterritorial rights. Individual figures like Namık Kemal and Shinasi Efendi poured their ideas into their own literary output, but they reached only a limited circle. However, their work was important in influencing those who came after them. Namık Kemal's melodramatic play *Vatan yahut Silistre (Fatherland or Silistria)*, first produced in 1873, became, after Abdul Hamid banned it, immensely popular with the students in the military schools, who smuggled copies back and forth under the noses of their instructors.

It is impossible to evaluate with any accuracy the extent of the influence of the ideas of western Europe on Turkey for any given period of time. Suffice it to say that the process of infiltration was steady throughout the reign of Abdul Aziz and that the circle of Turkish liberals was constantly widening. But the deposition of Abdul Aziz finally came, not through the initiative of the Young Turks (or New Ottomans), but from the recognition on the part of certain Turkish military and administrative officials that Abdul Aziz's excesses were on the verge of ruining the financial structure of the empire.

The leading figure in the move to depose Abdul Aziz in 1876 was Midhat Pasha, an extremely able Turkish official who began to make a name for himself in the 1860's as a provincial governor, first in European Turkey and then in Bagdad.[3] His enlightened policies resulted finally in the adoption of a completely new system of provincial government; that it never became effective was no fault of his.

In 1873 the Sultan, who was vaguely disturbed by such a display of energy, reluctantly called Midhat Pasha to Constantinople to become Grand Vizier. Abdul Aziz needed money, and he thought simply that Midhat Pasha might be able to wring

[3] On Midhat Pasha see Ali Haydar Midhat, *The Life of Midhat Pasha: A Record of his Services, Political Reforms, Banishment, and Judicial Murder* (London, 1903); Sir William Miller, *The Ottoman Empire and its Successors* (rev. and enlarged ed.; Cambridge, 1936), chap. xv; and Mehmed Zeki Pâkalin, *Midhat Paşa* (Istanbul, 1940).

more out of the country for him. On arriving in the capital, Midhat was immediately confronted with the necessity of making a choice. He could either close his eyes to the corruption and graft which pervaded the government, as his predecessors had done, or he could make an attempt to clean house as he had done in the provinces. He chose the latter course and plunged into an investigation of the finances of the government and of the Sultan's court.

Midhat's action produced a split in the government, and two parties began to take shape. The new Grand Vizier was on one side, supported by the most enlightened element of the empire. On the other stood the party of reaction, headed by Mahmut Nedim Pasha,[4] the former Grand Vizier who had been displaced by Midhat. This situation did not prevail for long, for Abdul Aziz, who wanted money, not investigations, decided that Midhat was causing altogether too much commotion and sent him off to Salonika as provincial governor once more.

In 1875-1876 the empire was confronted by troubles of a very serious nature. Bulgarian and Serbian nationalist aspirations, compounded by crop failures and Turkish misrule, led to open insurrection. Then, as a direct consequence of the Sultan's extravagances, the Ottoman government was forced to declare itself bankrupt. The first factor brought the threat of European interference to protect the Serbs and Bulgarians, who were being ruthlessly suppressed by the Turks; the second resulted in 1881 in the establishment of the international body known as the Administration of the Ottoman Public Debt.[5]

Midhat Pasha and others now felt that the government of the Ottoman Empire must be taken out of the hands of Abdul Aziz before the Ottoman Empire either collapsed or was torn apart by foreign powers. Midhat was a convinced constitution-

---

[4] Mehmed Zeki Pâkalin, *Mahmud Nedim Paşa* (Istanbul, 1940), is the only biography of this great rival of Midhat Pasha.

[5] Donald C. Blaisdell, *European Financial Control in the Ottoman Empire: A Study of the Establishment, Activities, and Significance of the Administration of the Ottoman Public Debt* (New York, 1929), p. 1.

alist, partly, as Sir Harry Luke says,[6] "because he was sufficiently shrewd and realistic a statesman to know that only by drastic internal reform, self administered, could the rapidly dissolving Empire stave off the coup de grâce which Russia was impatient to administer."

By the spring of the following year, Midhat Pasha had collected enough of a following to be able to depose Abdul Aziz. The New Ottomans, the Young Turks of that era, played little part in what was really only a palace revolution engineered by Midhat Pasha and one or two high-ranking army officers, although one of the members of the society, Ziya Pasha, was in on the coup d'état.

The Sultan who came now to the throne was Murat V, son of Abdul Mejid and nephew of Abdul Aziz. Unfortunately for the future of the Ottoman Empire, Murat, who, like all heirs-apparent to the Turkish throne, had been kept under close surveillance during the reign of his predecessor and encouraged to overindulge his taste for alcohol, was apparently mentally unstable. The series of events which resulted in his elevation to the throne seem to have terrified him, and when Abdul Aziz subsequently died under circumstances which are still surrounded by an unnecessary aura of mystery, Murat appears to have gone completely out of his mind.[7] Thus he in turn was deposed, for the reform party still had the upper hand and was determined to have a Sultan who would further their program. Murat's brief reign lasted only from May to August 1876, and he was succeeded by his brother, Abdul Hamid II, whose name was to become a synonym for iniquity.

Midhat Pasha and his supporters seemed at last to have found a ruler who would cooperate with them in an effort to revive

[6] *The Making of Modern Turkey: From Byzantium to Angora* (London, 1936), p. 123.

[7] Abdul Aziz almost unquestionably committed suicide with a pair of scissors; such at least was the verdict of the physicians attached to the various embassies in Constantinople, who were hurriedly called in to view the body. Later Abdul Hamid refused to accept this testimony when Midhat Pasha was "tried" for the alleged murder of Abdul Aziz.

the failing empire, and the events of the first few months of the new Sultan's reign tended to bear out their belief. The situation in the Balkans had deteriorated steadily to the point where Russia was on the verge of armed intervention. The Turks were forced to agree to a truce in the Balkans, and the European powers resolved to impose reforms on the Turkish government. For the purpose of drafting a program of reforms, a conference of ambassadors was convened in Constantinople, but on December 23, 1876, Abdul Hamid interrupted their labors by promulgating a constitution for the Ottoman Empire. The ambassadors were then politely told that their work was obviously no longer necessary. A parliament was summoned, and the Ottoman Empire appeared to be on the path marked out for it by the reform party.

However, Midhat Pasha had misjudged the new Sultan. On February 5, 1877, Midhat was unceremoniously dismissed from office and banished, for Abdul Hamid was not disposed to have near him the man who had already deposed two Sultans. On April 24 Russia, seeing no hope of obtaining the desired reforms peacefully and always looking for an opportunity to realize her historic ambitions in Constantinople, declared war on Turkey for the fourth time in the nineteenth century. In the following month the first parliament in the history of the Ottoman Empire was prorogued, not to meet again until 1908. The new Sultan had yielded to his liberal advisers only until he felt secure enough on his throne to dispense with them; for him the war with Russia was a godsend, for it provided him with an excuse to adjourn the parliament.

The war did little to solve the problems which had provoked it. Neither England nor Austria-Hungary was prepared to allow the Russians to enjoy the fruits of victory. Consequently, the Treaty of San Stefano, imposed on the Sultan by Russia, was negated by the Congress of Berlin in the summer of 1878. A series of compromises aimed at preserving the status quo was worked out. Russia was forced to reward herself at the expense of Rumania; Bosnia and Herzegovina were turned over to

Austrian administration; and Great Britain took over the responsibility for Cyprus. The Bulgarians and Serbs had to content themselves with halfway solutions of their nationalist aspirations.

As far as Abdul Hamid was concerned, he had gained his own ends and had come as well out of a bad situation as he could have hoped for. He now felt strong enough to continue in the course of absolutism, and until 1908 he was able to do so.

Abdul Hamid made a good first impression both in his own country and abroad. For some years there was no opposition from his subjects to his rule, and foreign observers were almost unanimous in their praise of the new Sultan. Disraeli wrote to Salisbury, "The new Sultan really promises. Will he be a Solyman the Great?"[8] Even in the last decade of the nineteenth century a popular writer could say of him, "His rare industry, his unexampled economy, his steadfastness of purpose, and his moral courage, have won for him the affection of his subjects, and the commendation of foreigners who visit his capital."[9]

An abrupt halt was finally brought to these eulogies by the Armenian massacres of the 1890's. Like other nationalities embraced by the Ottoman Empire, the Armenians were beginning to develop a national consciousness. Many Armenians fled the country and began to agitate for an Armenian national state. Revolutionary societies were formed within the empire. After a number of relatively minor skirmishes, the Armenian revolutionaries organized a large scale uprising in 1894. They were fully conscious that the Turks would take drastic action in return, but they were prepared to sacrifice their own people in order to attract the attention of the European powers to their desires.

The Turks, taking the not unnatural view that they were dealing with an internal rebellion, put down the uprising with despatch. However, they went too far: some ten to twenty

[8] Quoted in Philip P. Graves, *Briton and Turk* (London, 1941), p. 30.
[9] Elizabeth Wormeley Latimer, *Russia and Turkey in the Nineteenth Century* (Chicago, 1893), p. 343.

thousand Armenians were massacred by Kurdish irregular troops organized somewhat like the Russian Cossacks.

In 1896 a band of Armenian terrorists seized the Ottoman Bank in the Galata quarter of Constantinople, killing a number of persons in the process. They were prepared to murder everyone in the bank and hold out until foreign attention had been attracted. To prevent further bloodshed, the Turkish government permitted the terrorists, who had meantime lost their courage, to escape, but in the course of the next two days five or six thousand Armenians were massacred by mobs in Constantinople. The massacres were on a highly selective basis, since no other minorities were molested, and the government looked the other way.

These were only the principal manifestations of a situation which lasted for some years. The severity with which the Armenians were treated cannot be condoned, but it is equally difficult to condone the coldblooded calculation with which the Armenian revolutionaries deliberately offered up thousands of their people in a vain attempt to achieve their ends. Many of those who died were not even aware of what was happening.[10]

In any event, Abdul Hamid speedily acquired a far different reputation abroad from that with which he had begun his reign. Particularly in England and America public opinion became inflamed against the Turks, and to the Sultan the strongest possible epithets were applied. By 1897 Richard Davey was writing in his book, *The Sultan and his Subjects*,[11]

A year or so ago, Sultan Abd-ul-Hamid appeared to be earnestly striving against cruel odds, to do what was best for his people. But recent events demand a change of opinion. The good he has done is drowned—drowned in the blood of countless murdered men, women, and children, and, in the lurid light of these scenes of horror,

[10] On the still highly controversial Armenian question see William L. Langer, *The Diplomacy of Imperialism* (New York, 1935), vol. I, chaps. v and x, which provide an objective and carefully documented account. Langer demonstrates conclusively that the massacres were deliberately provoked by the Armenian revolutionaries.

[11] (New York, 1897), vol. I, p. 197.

he takes on the semblance of some loathsome spider, caught in the silken web of his own Hareem, and condemned there to re-incarnate the most evil of his ancestors, whose very names conjure up dread memories of murder and rapine.

Actually, foreign opinion was very late in undergoing revision. Turkish liberal spirits had long since realized Abdul Hamid's true nature, for in the years after the war with Russia, the Sultan did everything in his power to seal the borders of the empire hermetically against western European influences. Midhat Pasha had been brought back to Constantinople and tried for the "murder" of Abdul Aziz, found guilty, and sentenced to death. He had been spared through the intercession of the foreign ambassadors, but he was subsequently strangled while in exile in Arabia. Abdul Hamid meantime moved into the famous palace, Yildiz, surrounded by high walls on the heights overlooking the Bosphorus, and there he sat for the rest of his reign, concerned only with the problem of maintaining himself on the throne. His whole reign was devoted to that end. The notorious espionage system which made every man a spy on his neighbor, the policy of exiling anyone who disagreed with him, the practice of allowing his servants to enrich themselves at public expense so that they would remain faithful to him; in short, the entire Hamidian system, had but one aim: the security of the Sultan himself.

Abdul Hamid has been described as a man of consummate skill in the game of playing off opposing forces, internal and external, against one another. Much has been written about his ability to frustrate the designs of the European powers, for example, by spinning his intrigues so that the powers counterbalanced one another. But this view of the Sultan belongs in the realm of mythology along with the countless legends which have grown up around his private life. The conflicting interests of the European powers were already there; no stimulus was needed from Abdul Hamid to persuade England to block Russian ambitions at the straits. And Abdul Hamid himself was such a mass of contradictions that he never followed any definite policy; he was more inclined, for example, to follow the suggestions of his astrologer, Ebül Huda, than to work out his own decisions.[12]

Arminius Vambéry, the Hungarian scholar who knew Abdul Hamid as well as any European ever knew him, has left us the following picture of the strange master of Yildiz:

> I never met with a man the salient features of whose character were so contradictory, so uneven and disproportionate, as with Sultan Abdul Hamid. Benevolence and wickedness, generosity and meanness, cowardice and valour, shrewdness and ignorance, moderation and excess and many, many other qualities have alternately found expression in his acts and words. If there was a predominant feature in his character it was his timidity, the constant wavering and the apprehension of having committed a wrong step, which left an indelible mark upon all his doings. This unfortunate quality, the disastrous effect of harem education, frustrated his best intentions; it blunted his otherwise splendid mental capacities and made his reign a misfortune to his country.[13]

The spirit which had produced the first Young Turk movement was by no means dead, but for the first decade of his reign and more Abdul Hamid was not troubled by any organized movement against himself and his policies.[14] For a time, then, it was felt that Abdul Hamid would use the absolute power he had taken into his hands for the good of the country, and the liberals demonstrated that they were more nationalistic than liberal by condoning his abandonment of constitutional government on those grounds. But as it came to be realized that Abdul Hamid was interested only in himself and that his reign bade

[12] So, at least, say European sources. Dr. Adnan Adıvar of Istanbul, a very well-informed man, questioned this point, however.

[13] "Personal Recollections of Abdul Hamid and his Court," *Nineteenth Century*, LXVI (July 1909), p. 69.

[14] Ali Suavi Efendi, who had been a member of the *Yeni Osmanlılar* and who had published the Young Turk journal *Mukhbir* (The *"Advertiser"* or *"Informer"*) in London during the 1860's, made an attempt on May 20, 1878, to rescue Murat V from Chiragan Palace, where he was held in seclusion by Abdul Hamid. However, Ali Suavi and his handful of followers were not acting on behalf of a widespread Young Turk organization, and the abortive attempt only served to confirm the Sultan in his path of reaction.

fair to be a reversion to the darkest days of the old empire rather than a step forward, the opposition began to develop once more. With the development of this new resistance movement were laid the seeds of the Young Turk Revolution of 1908, for despite numerous setbacks, betrayals, and disappointments, the thread can be traced from the end of the 1880's to 1908.

CHAPTER II

The First Phase—Birth of the Committee of Union and Progress—The Young Turk Movement in Turkey and Abroad—The Collapse of the Committee of Union and Progress in 1897

IN THE year 1889 a group of students at the Imperial Military Medical School in Constantinople formed a revolutionary organization for the express purpose of overthrowing Abdul Hamid II, the Sultan of the Ottoman Empire and the Caliph or spiritual head of Islam for a good share of the world's Moslems.[1]

Appropriately enough, the *Mektebi Tıbbiyeyi Askeriye*, or Military Medical School, was located at that time squarely between *Top Kapı Sarayı*, the Seraglio of the Ottoman Sultans, and the Sirkeji railroad station. In the preceding year the first through train from Paris had entered this station, and it was largely from Paris that Western ideas were commencing to seep into the Ottoman Empire.

The driving spirit behind the formation of this group, which marks the real beginning of the Young Turk movement against Abdul Hamid, was an Albanian named Ibrahim Temo, or Edhem, as he was sometimes called. Temo, who had been a student at the school for several years, had been given ample opportunity to discover a number of kindred spirits, particularly in the preceding year, when the student body had gone on strike against the administration of the school.[2] The Palace had,

---

[1] There is a considerable difference of opinion among the various authorities concerning the exact date of the founding of the organization. In accepting 1889, I am following particularly the memoirs of the founder of the society, İbrahim Temo, *İttihad ve Terakki Cemiyetinin Teşekülü ve Hidematı Vataniye ve İnkılâbı Milliye Dair Hatıratım* [*The Formation of the Society of Union and Progress and my Memories respecting Services to the Fatherland and the National Revolution*] (Medjidia, Rumania, 1939), p. 18. See also the article "Abdülhamid II," *İslam Ansiklopedisi*, vol. 1, p. 78.

[2] Ibrahim Temo, *op.cit.*, pp. 14-15.

at that time, asked for a list of the strikers, but the administration, not daring to admit that the whole student body was involved, had submitted the names of only 32 of the 340 students. Nevertheless, this was enough to give the school a bad name with the Sultan.

In May 1889 Temo approached three fellow students whose views were already well known to him, Ishak Sükûti, Cherkes Mehmet Reshit, and Abdullah Jevdet, with the suggestion that they form a secret patriotic society.[3] These four students became the nucleus of an organization which soon began to attract other students. In a short time the original quadrumvirate was joined by such men as Sherefeddin Magmumî, Giritli Shefik, Jevdet Osman, Kerim Sebâti, Mekkeli Sabri, and Selânikli Nazim.[4] The last named individual, who achieved some notoriety at the time of the Revolution of 1908, was, like Talât Pasha, one of the few men to bridge the gap between this early group and the later Committee of Union and Progress.

The organization of the society was patterned after that of the Italian Carbonari of the earlier part of the century. Temo, during the summer vacation in the year before he founded the society, had stopped over at Brindisi while en route by sea to his home in Albania. During his stay in Brindisi and in Naples, Temo visited a Freemasonic lodge in company with a friend and learned enough about the role of the Carbonari in Italian history and their organization to influence him later on when he decided to start a similar secret society in Turkey.[5]

[3] *ibid.*, pp. 16-18. Ahmed Bedevi Kuran, *Inkılâp Tarihimiz ve İttihad ve Terakki* (Istanbul, 1948), p. 61, adds one Hüseyin zade Ali from Baku to this list. He also notes that some authorities include the names of Hikmet Emin and İsmail İbrahim.

[4] Because of the fact that family names were virtually unknown in Turkey at this time, it was a common practice to identify a man by giving him some sort of nickname or by coupling his name with the place to which he was native. Thus Sherefeddin Magmumî means "Sherefeddin the Gloomy"; "Giritli" identifies Shefik as a native of Crete; "Mekkeli" indicates that Sabri came from Mecca; "Selânikli" shows that Nazim was a resident of Salonika; and "Cherkes" demonstrates that Mehmet Reshit was a Circassian.

[5] Letter of Fehmi Janer dated March 25, 1941; letter of the late Dr. Akil Muhtar Özden, dated May 4, 1941. For an explanation of the nature of these

The Carbonari influence is evident in this first Young Turk committee, which was apparently called "Progress and Union" (*Terakki ve İttihat*) rather than "Union and Progress" (*İttihat ve Terakki*), the name under which the society was to become so well known later on,[6] in that the members were supposed to be known to each other only as numerical fractions. These fractions were formed by numbering each new cell of the organization and then giving a number to each member of that group. The number of the cell or branch served as the denominator of the fraction and the number of the individual member as the numerator. To illustrate, the fifth member of the seventh cell was entered on the lists of the society simply as "5/7." Ibrahim Temo, as the founder of the movement, was "1/1."[7]

With deadly seriousness the young conspirators held their first gatherings, to each of which they subsequently assigned a name. The first meeting was labelled "The Meeting of the Four" (*Dörtler İçtimaı*), and the next few were called "The Woodstack Reading-Room Meetings" *Hatab Kiraathanesi İçtimaları*).[8] Then, a month or two after the first meeting, the members assembled at a coffee-house outside the Adrianople Gate in the old walls of Constantinople. Twelve men attended this "Meeting under the Fig Tree" (*İnciraltı İçtimaı*), which was the first formal gathering of the new society, the others

---

letters and others cited below, see the bibliographical essay at the end of the book. Janer specifically notes that he had this story from Temo in 1908, but Temo does not mention his Italian visit in his memoirs.

[6] Janer, *loc. cit.*

[7] Letter of Fazlı Tung, dated May 20, 1941. See also Paul Fesch, *Constantinople aus derniers Jours d'Abdul-Hamid* (Paris, 1907), p. 330. Fesch also states that each member knew only the person who initiated him and the member who brought him his instructions from the committee; Akil Muhtar Özden, *loc. cit.*, says that each member was acquainted with five others. Actually it would appear that any such rule could not have been enforced easily, as the student lived in such close quarters. Temo, *op. cit.*, p. 20, remarks only that he was designated in the society as "1/1."

[8] Temo, *op. cit.*, pp. 19-21. See also, K. Süssheim, " 'Abd Allah Djewdet," *Encyclopedia of Islam, Supplement* (1938), p. 56; this account is quite detailed on the early meetings. Fazlı Tung, *loc. cit.*, says only that the students used to sit on the woodstack near the bath and discuss the organization of the society.

having been merely hurried and surreptitious conferences between classes. Present, according to Temo,[9] were, in addition to himself, the following men: Ishak Sükûti, Sherefeddin Mag-mumî, Abdullah Jevdet, Cherkes Mehmet Reshit, Assaf Dervish, Hersekli (Herzegovinian) Ali Rushdi, described by Temo as a "high official," Muharrem Girid, an instructor in the medical school, and three others whose names Temo has forgotten.[10]

These twelve elected officers as their first order of business and then drew up a program, the details of which none of them has seen fit to pass on to us. Ali Rushdi, because of his age and position, was elected president, while Sherefeddin was made secretary and Assaf Dervish treasurer. Temo, the real founder of the movement, was not elected to office, but retained his numerical designation in the society as "1/1."[11]

Members taken in subsequent to this meeting included Kosovalı Ibrahim Efendi, Nejip Draga, Shatin Bey, and a postal official named Talât who was to become a member of the notorious triumvirate which ruled Turkey a number of years later.

Within the Military Medical School the movement spread rapidly and soon overflowed into the other government higher schools in Constantinople, such as the Military Academy (*Harbiye Mektebi*), the Veterinary School (*Baytariye*), the Civil College (*Mülkiye*), which was a school for training government officials, the Naval Academy (*Bahriye*), and the

---

[9] Temo, *loc. cit.*

[10] Inasmuch as Temo's memoirs were published fifty years after these events, it is not surprising that there are a few gaps in his memory. The three unnamed individuals may well have been any of those mentioned as early members of the society by other sources.

[11] Temo, *loc. cit.* See also the excellent article by General-major z. D. Imhoff, "Die Entstehung und der Zweck des Comités für Einheit und Fortschritt," *Die Welt des Islams*, I (1913), pp. 171-172. Imhoff's article consists of miscellaneous information which he collected while it was still fresh in the minds of the participants with the hope that it would serve as a starting point for the future historian of the movement. He was a very reliable observer, for his information checks almost perfectly with the accounts of Temo and others.

Artillery and Engineering School (*Topçu ve Mühendishane*).[12]

One is immediately inclined to ask why the standard of revolt against Abdul Hamid was first raised by the military cadets. The explanation is simple: first of all, the influence of the West was felt by the younger men primarily, those who had not yet been stamped by the pattern of their fathers; secondly, it was not possible for this susceptible generation to obtain an adequate education anywhere in the country except in the military schools. The University of Constantinople was not founded until 1900, and was then the only one in the country.[13] Under Abdul Hamid it was allowed so little freedom that its instruction was stereotyped and limited to such subjects as the censorship permitted.

The only other schools which might conceivably be called institutions of higher learning were the theological seminaries, the *medreses*, and they gave a one-sided education, to say the least. Thus the military schools, maintained at a comparatively high level in keeping with Ottoman military tradition, became, paradoxically enough, the Achilles' heel of the ruler who wanted only to be protected. From what or whom he wanted to be protected was probably never clear even to him, but he did allow foreigners to come in and take his army in hand. Thus he exposed his officer-candidates to the influences of the West—which he rigorously excluded from his empire in every other respect insofar as that was possible.[14]

[12] See, in addition to the previously cited letters of Fazlı Tung and Fehmi Janer, the letters of Ömer Fevzi Mardin, dated March 4, 1941, and of Nahit Kervan, undated; the latter notes that when he was a student in the Artillery School in 1896-1897 only ten to twelve per cent of the students belonged to the society, which was "much more widespread" at the *Harbiye*, or Military Academy, and especially at the Military Medical School.

[13] Paul Monroe, "Education," in Eliot Grinnell Mears, *Modern Turkey* (New York, 1924), p. 125. It should be pointed out that Istanbul University, as it is now called, can actually trace its descent in one form or another to the sixteenth Century, although there were various occasions when the continuity was broken.

[14] See Lieutenant-colonel Malleterre, "L'Armée jeune-turque," *Revue des Sciences Politiques*, XXVI (September, 1911), pp. 734-755, and especially pp. 737-739 on the military schools and their influence.

In the Ottoman Empire there were not very many careers open to young men of good family. It was generally a choice between one branch or another of the government service that had to be made, so they entered the army or became govern ment officials. Consequently the young intelligentsia of the empire were to be found in the schools to which we have been referring, and the original four were worthy representatives of this group. Abdullah Jevdet, for example, became a qualified doctor in 1894 and immediately began to publish medical works which made him some reputation in this field.[15] He also became known as a translator, for he industriously put into Turkish works from French, Italian, English, German, and Persian literature. One of his greatest contributions was the translation of many of Shakespeare's works into Turkish.[16]

All of the young revolutionaries were steeped in the works of the proscribed nationalist poets, Namık Kemal, Shinasi, and Ziya Pasha. Ishak Sükûti was especially well acquainted with the writings of Namık Kemal, whose ideas he spread with great zeal. One gathers, however, that these ideas were already rather widespread, for one Turkish gentleman who joined the society in 1895 notes that even when he was in secondary school the students used to meet in the school garden to discuss the for-bidden writers and such other dangerous topics as the deposition of Murat.[17]

Within a relatively short time—probably in 1892, although it is difficult to be exact—the existence of the society became known to Abdul Hamid.[18] According to the late Dr. Akil Muhtar Özden, whose account of this period is quite detailed, three "morally weak" students made a report (*jurnal*) to the palace that "ideas of liberty" were circulating freely throughout

[15] Süssheim, *op. cit.*, p. 55.
[16] See Otto Hachtmann, "Abdullah Dschewdet als Übersetzer," *Islamische Welt*, I (1917), pp. 526-529. All of Abdullah Jevdet's translations from European literature were apparently done from French versions.
[17] Akil Muhtar Özden, *loc. cit.*
[18] *idem*; Fazlı Tung, *loc. cit.*; letter of Ali Osman Onbulak, dated March 20, 1941; Süssheim, *op. cit.*, p. 56, states definitely that it was 1892.

the Military Medical School.[19] In any event, the Sultan reacted violently. Ali Saip Pasha, the commandant of the school, was relieved of his duties, and Zeki Pasha, the director of the military schools, was put in charge with instructions to stamp out the conspiracy. A number of the students were grilled, but only a few were finally taken into custody, including Abdullah Jevdet, Giritli Shefik, and Sherefeddin Magmumî. Subsequently, some fourteen more were arrested when they protested against the confinement of their fellow students.[20] Apparently this first stage of the conspiracy was not taken very seriously, however, as we know that Abdullah Jevdet was allowed to complete his course of study and that he resumed his work against the Sultan.

In the meantime, the society kept on growing and now entered into a new phase of its existence by commencing to seek adherents outside the schools. In the first phase of its activity the society had decided to restrict its proselytizing to the students in the government schools in Constantinople, although it was recognized that there would be some dissemination of ideas among the younger relatives of the members, but now the time seemed to be ripe for expansion into the population of the city. A particularly fertile field might seem to have been offered by the *medreses,* or theological schools, which were to be found in conjunction with most of the large mosques, for the number of *softas,* or theological students, was enormous.[21] However, while the *softas* were often a source of trouble for the govern-

---

[19] Akil Muhtar Özden, *loc. cit.*; Fazlı Tung, *loc. cit.*, says only that the society was betrayed by the irresponsible talk of some of the members who had become too bold.

[20] Akil Muhtar Özden, *loc. cit.*

[21] Fehmi Janer, *loc. cit.*, states that there were 30,000 *softas* at this time. The *softas* were certainly regarded with suspicion by the government. Sir Charles Eliot, *Turkey in Europe* (new ed., London, 1908), pp. 180-181, says of them, "There are many thousands of them in such religious centres as Constantinople and Konia, but the reason why most of them have adopted this learned profession is not by any means a passion for theology, but a desire to escape military service . . ." He continues, "These large houses of fanatical and ignorant men, mostly between the ages of twenty and forty, without regular employment, are a constant source of danger, and are sometimes disbanded by the government." See also Richard Davey, *The Sultan and his Subjects* (New York, 1897), I, pp. 78-79.

ment, they were by no means good potential material for the Young Turk movement. Indeed, it was the *softas* who formed the backbone of the abortive counter-revolution of 1909.

It is again impossible to give an exact date to the beginning of the program of expansion. We can only say that in the two or three years prior to 1896 a number of prominent men joined the society and that the leadership commenced to pass into their hands. Chief among these men were Haji Ahmet Efendi,[22] a civil servant in the bureau of accounting of the *Seraskerat* (War Office), and a dervish *Sheyh* named Naili Efendi.[23] Both were influential men with entree to many circles in Constantinople, and under their guidance the society soon acquired a considerable following among the more enlightened element in the city. It seems probable that many of their supporters came from the remnants of an earlier group of Young Turks, the "*Yeni Osmanlılar*"—literally, "New Ottomans"—of Abdul Aziz's day, for Sheyh Naili is reported to have been one of the founders of that group.[24]

In the Military Medical School the leadership of the society had passed into the hands of Mekkeli Sabri, who worked particularly with Haji Ahmet to spread the ideas of the organization. The work was maintained in the schools as well, but a number of the older students who had come under suspicion were now finding it expedient to leave the country, and in 1894-1895 a steady trickle of these members escaped to Europe, where they concentrated, for the most part, in Paris. Those who could afford it went for a double purpose—to escape the vengeance of the Sultan and to further their studies. In this category was Selânikli Nazim, who managed to complete his medical

[22] The title "Haji" (Pilgrim) is given anyone who has made the pilgrimage to Mecca.

[23] Fehmi Janer states that Naili was associated with the dervish cloister or monastery known as "Chaylak" (Kite or Hawk), but I have never been able to locate a cloister of this name. However, Dr. Adnan Adıvar of Istanbul informed me that Naili was a member of the Bedevi order.

[24] Fehmi Janer states that Naili, together with the Vezir Sami Pashazade and Ayetullah Bey, founded the *Yeni Osmanlılar*.

education in France while carrying on the struggle against Abdul Hamid.

In Paris the young conspirators found that a small colony of liberal Turks had already assembled, including Halil Ganem, a Christian Syrian from Beirut who had been a delegate from Syria to the first Turkish parliament in 1878. Ganem had fled to Europe after Abdul Hamid had prorogued the parliament and had founded in Paris a journal called *La Jeune Turquie*. Previously he had published another paper in Geneva, the *Hilâl* (Crescent), but inasmuch as these ventures were not self-supporting, he also wrote for various publications, particularly the *Journal des Débats* until that paper took sides with "the Sultan's government and a financial syndicate."[25]

In 1889 the Paris colony was joined by Ahmet Riza, who was to be the best-known of the Young Turks of Europe. Son of an Austrian mother,[26] and a father known because of his Anglophile tendencies as "Ingiliz Ali Bey," Ahmet Riza had been given a liberal education, partly in France, and he spoke and wrote the French language to perfection. In appearance he was as far from the general European conception of a Turk as possible. He was tall and spare with a neatly trimmed beard and a severe countenance which gave some indication of the corresponding severity of his character. No one ever questioned his singleness of purpose, his idealism, or his uncompromising honesty. For all that

[25] Karl Blind, "Young Turkey," *Fortnightly Review*, LXVI (December, 1896), p. 836. On Halil Ganem see also, Blind's "The Prorogued Turkish Parliament," *North American Review*, CLXXV (July, 1902), p. 44; Heinrich Zimmerer, "Die Europäische Türkei und Armenien," in *Helmolt's Weltgeschichte* (Leipzig and Vienna, 1905), vol. v, p. 188; Fesch, *op. cit.*, pp. 313, 316, 321, 324-325, etc.; Hans Kohn, "Der arabische Nationalismus," *Zeitschrift für Politik*, XVII (1927), p. 29; and the unpublished letters of Dr. Ali Osman Onbulak and Fazlı Tung cited above.

[26] There is some disagreement on this point, some writers maintaining that Riza's mother was Hungarian. K. Süssheim, in "Der Zusammenbruch des türkischen Reiches in Europa," *Veröffentlichungen der Handelshochschule München*, vol. III, *Die Balkanfrage* (Munich, 1914), p. 91, even goes so far as to state that Riza's father was English, but this is obviously a misinterpretation of "Ingiliz" Ali Bey's nickname. Haluk Y. Şehsuvaroğlu, writing in the Istanbul newspaper *Cumhuriyet* on January 26, 1950, states that Ahmet Riza's mother was an Austrian who embraced Islam.

he was a singularly unpopular man with his fellow Young Turks, for he was just as unyielding and dogmatic in his convictions as he was in matters affecting his personal integrity.[27]

These convictions had finally led Ahmet Riza to leave his position as director of public instruction in the Vilayet of Hudavendigâr (Bursa) and carry on a campaign against the government of Abdul Hamid from a vantage point outside the Empire. Shortly after Selânikli Nazım arrived in Paris, he approached Ahmet Riza with the suggestion that he become the director of a journal which was to be the official organ of the society. In this manner Ahmet Riza became affiliated with the organization and commenced, late in 1895, in conjunction with Halil Ganem and a number of other exiles, to publish the paper *Mechveret*[28] (*Consultation* or *Deliberation*) which was to appear twice a month. It was to be published in Turkish only, as it was intended for readers inside the Ottoman Empire, but Ahmet Riza took it upon himself to add a French supplement.[29]

At one time or another Riza had been attracted by the philosophy of Auguste Comte, and he soon became a familiar figure in Positivist circles in Paris as well as an occasional contributor to the *Revue Occidentale*, the publication of the French Positivists. It is interesting to note the account given by that periodical of the founding of *Mechveret*:

> We call to the attention of our readers the appearance of a new journal MECHVERET (*la Consultation*), organ of Young Turkey, published in the Arabic [*sic*] language, with a French supplement, under the direction of M. Ahmed Riza.

[27] On Ahmet Riza see especially the articles by Blind cited above; Fesch, *op. cit.*, chapter "La Jeune Turquie," *passim*; Baron [Bernard] Carra de Vaux, *Les Penseurs de l'Islam* (Paris, 1921-1926), vol. 5, pp. 159ff.; John Macdonald, *Turkey and the Eastern Question* (London and New York [1913]), pp. 54-55; and the unpublished letters of Dr. Akil Muhtar Özden, Rahmi Bey, Fehmi Janer, Dr. Ali Osman Onbulak, and Fazlı Tung.

[28] I have retained the French spelling here inasmuch as the paper was widely known by that title. A better English transliteration of the modern Turkish spelling (*Meşveret*) would be *Meshveret*.

[29] Fesch, *op. cit.*, p. 335.

MECHVERET, which bears the Positivist date, appears twice a month, with our device *Order and Progress.*[30]

Thus it may be seen that while *Mechveret* was the official organ of the Committee of Union and Progress, it was from the start to a great extent appropriated by Ahmet Riza as his own personal property, for with the possible exception of Halil Ganem, none of his associates was a follower of Comte. Riza's refusal to compromise his personal ideas in the slightest for the sake of general amity in the party was one of the chief causes of the rift which was soon to appear in the society, but this same quality later carried him proudly through a period when all around him were succumbing to the blandishments of the sultan.[31]

Under the date "27 Frédéric 107" (December 3, 1895)[32] *Mechveret* set forth the aims of the society for its readers. Inasmuch as this statement contains the first complete exposition of the views of the organization it has been thought advisable to reproduce it in full at this point. The article is headed "Our Program" and reads as follows:

The Ottoman Committee of Union and Progress has just founded in Paris a journal *Mechveret* (the Consultation), with a view to manifesting its existence, the press being, as is known, muzzled in Turkey.

A French supplement will put foreign readers au courant of the tendencies and desires of the Young Turk party.

The program which follows explains with great clarity the line of conduct which we have traced for ourselves and the goal which we wish to attain.

[30] *Revue Occidentale*, sec. sér., XII (January, 1896), p. 127. Midhat Pasha had been welcomed and honored by the Positivists of Paris when he was exiled in 1878. See *Revue Occidentale*, 1re année (September and November, 1878), pp. 511ff. and 630ff.

[31] See below.

[32] Riza even went so far as to use the Positivist calendar to date *Mechveret*. This calendar used January 1, 1789 as its starting point, and its months, weeks, and even days were named after the men Comte considered to be the most important in the history of the world. Of these, the thirteen most important gave their names to the months. Riza did make use of the Gregorian date as well but ignored the Moslem calendar, an omission which increased his unpopularity.

We have assured ourselves of the collaboration of certain personalities whose ardent desire is to see the former bonds of harmony and good friendship with the Ottomans taken up again and renewed.

We wish to work not to overthrow the reigning dynasty, which we consider necessary to the maintenance of good order, but to propagate the notion of progress of which we desire the peaceful triumph. Our motto being "Order and Progress," we have a horror of concessions obtained by violence.

We demand reforms, not especially for this or that province, but for the entire Empire, not in favor of a single nationality, but in favor of all the Ottomans, be they Jews, Christians, or Moslems.

We wish to advance in the path of civilization, but we declare resolutely, we do not wish to advance other than in fortifying the Ottoman element and in respecting its own conditions of existence.

We are determined to guard the originality of our oriental civilization and, for this reason, to borrow from the Occident only the general results of their scientific evolution, only the things truly assimilable and necessary to guide a people in its march towards liberty.

There are, in Europe, men of heart, who, disengaged from all fanaticism, have nothing in view but the common good of the Occident and the Orient; it is from them that we hope for moral support.

We are opposed to the substitution of direct intervention by the foreign powers for Ottoman authority. This is not from fanaticism, because, for us, the religious question is a private affair—but from a legitimate sentiment of civil and national dignity.[33]

This program is clearly more the work of Ahmet Riza than of the society in general. He and his associates were in agreement on one fundamental point—the necessity of "Ottomanizing" the inhabitants of the empire—and this point remained the one unshakable plank in the platform of the Young Turks of a later day, despite the opposition views of certain elements.[34] Riza was speaking for himself, however, when he said, "Our motto being 'Order and Progress,' we have a horror of concessions obtained by violence." At the very moment that he was writing a coup was being planned in Constantinople by the

[33] Reproduced in *Revue Occidentale*, sec. sér., XII, p. 128.
[34] See below, chap. II, for a discussion of the various schools of Young Turk thought.

society, and it is now necessary to turn our attention once more to the development of the society within the empire.

In Constantinople the movement was spreading apace. From time to time the government became suspicious enough to make a few arrests, but the main body of conspirators remained intact for the time being. Late in 1895 several of the original members of the society, including Abdullah Jevdet, Ishak Sükûti, Sherefeddin Magmumî, and Kerim Sebâti were taken into custody and exiled. Sükûti, together with Chürüksulu (i.e. "from Chürüksu") Ahmet Bey, a teacher at the *Harbiye*, was exiled to Rhodes, whence the pair managed to escape and make their way to Paris.[35] Abdullah Jevdet was sent to Tripoli in Africa but eventually was able to slip over the border into Tunisia; he finally arrived in France in the summer of 1897.[36] Ibrahim Temo got out of the country before he could be arrested and went to Rumania, where he organized a branch of the society and published a Young Turk paper.[37]

This outbreak of arrests appears to have been precipitated by three main factors. First of all *Mechveret* was beginning to make its appearance in Turkey through the foreign post offices, which enjoyed extraterritorial privileges and were much used by the Young Turks at this time as well as later.[38] The circulation of this journal within the empire helped to make known the presence of some sort of a revolutionary society to the authorities. Second, the membership of the organization was so great that "all Istanbul thus became aware of the existence of a society,"[39] although no one was able to say who its members were or where they met. Even women were passing on countless exaggerated stories of the plans of the group, and the result was that the palace eventually began to start attaching some importance to the rumors.

---

[35] Letters of Dr. Akil Muhtar Özden and Fehmi Janer.
[36] Temo, *op. cit.*, pp. 61 ff.   [37] Letter of Janer.
[38] "Il est plus facile d'envoyer un journal de Paris à Erzeroum que de Péra à Galata." Paul Fesch, *Constantinople aux derniers jours d'Abdul-Hamid*, p. 328.
[39] Letter of Fehmi Janer.

Finally, one Murat Bey, a teacher of history at the *Mülkiye*, or Civil College, who had been brought into the society by Sheyh Naili,[40] chose this time to draw up a list of reforms he deemed necessary for the empire and to present it, unsolicited, to the palace. Like Ahmet Riza, he then considered it expedient to remove himself to a safe distance, in this case Egypt,[41] where, at the behest of the society, he founded another anti-Hamidian journal, *Mizan* (*Scales* or *Balance*), the name of which was carried over from a paper Murat had been editing in Constantinople. Thus another leader of Young Turk opinion emerged, and the government, enraged by this new assault on its dignity, arrested all of Murat's known associates.

Murat Bey was not by origin a Turk. He was born in Daghestan in the Caucasus and was probably educated in St. Petersburg.[42] While still a young man he made his way to Constantinople, presumably because of his feelings that as a Moslem his opportunities were greater there, although it may well be that he found Tsarist Russian government in the Caucasus unbearable or even that he was forced to flee his native land. For a time he was employed by the Council of the Public Debt, and eventually he was appointed to the faculty of the *Mülkiye*. In

---

[40] *idem.*

[41] The role of Egypt in the Young Turk struggle is a strange one. The Khedives of Egypt were nominally under the suzerainty of the Turkish Sultans, but the relationship lost much of its significance after the British occupied Egypt in 1881. Abbas Hilmi, who became Khedive in 1892, attempted to make the bond a more real one and visited Constantinople several times during the first years of his reign. However, Abdul Hamid soon succeeded in estranging the young Khedive, who thereafter vacillated between offering hospitality to the Young Turks and putting pressure on them to leave. Wilfrid Scawen Blunt gives an extremely interesting conversation with the Khedive in his diary in an entry of December 16, 1895, a conversation which demonstrates how astoundingly bad a statesman Abdul Hamid was (*My Diaries; Being a Personal Narrative of Events 1888-1914* [1 vol. edn., New York, 1932], pp. 207-209).

[42] Franz Babinger, *Die Geschichtsschreiber der Osmanen und ihre Werke* (Leipzig, 1927), p. 391, and letter of Fazlı Tung. With all due respect to Babinger's important work, it might be pointed out that his information on Murat is erroneous in part. For example, Babinger states that Murat did not return to the country until 1908 after leaving in 1895. Actually, Murat gave up the struggle and returned in 1897, as will be shown below.

the literary field Murat was extremely active. Among his endeavors was a *General History* in six volumes, which he followed with a one volume *Ottoman History*. These works having given him some reputation, he tried another tack and produced a semi-autobiographical novel entitled *Turfandamı yoksa Turfamı*, which might be translated freely as *First Fruits or Forbidden Fruits?*[43] In addition he found time to edit his paper *Mizan*, which activity brought him into conflict with the authorities from time to time.

From his writings, particularly *Turfandamı yoksa Turfamı*, which was somewhat nationalistic in tone, as well as from his work in the society, Murat developed a great following in the organization. On the other hand, the program of reforms which Murat demanded of the Sultan did little to enhance his reputation, for it was felt that his suggestions were far too shallow to have any significance.[44] Nevertheless, he left the country with the blessing of the society and the prayers of its members that he would be greatly instrumental in the work of undermining Abdul Hamid.

Meanwhile the arrests made by the government served only to increase the determination of the revolutionaries. The palace appears to have relaxed its vigilance somewhat after these last arrests, and the society correspondingly became a bit overconfident. As Fazlı Tung remarks,[45] "For example, we were sure that all of the high officials of the country known to be men of honor were in the society." Murat was even believed to have

---

[43] Bernhard Stern, *Jungtürken und Verschwörer* (2nd edn., Leipzig, 1901), p. 213, pictures Murat as arriving in Constantinople penniless and knowing no Turkish. This is possibly true, but if it is, it is difficult to understand how he acquired enough Turkish to become so adept as his literary outpourings indicate. It is also possible that he came from an area where Turkish of a sort was spoken. In Daghestan "inhabitants of adjacent valleys are apt to speak entirely different tongues. . ." (Sir Harry Luke, *More Moves on an Eastern Chequerboard* [London, 1935], p. 90), and in the Caucasus in general a great deal of Turkish is spoken.

[44] Letter of Fazlı Tung, according to whom Murat merely demanded a slight enlargement in the powers of the *Shurayı Devlet*, or Council of State, and certain budgetary reforms. According to Tung, Murat ascribed most of the ills which beset the country to carelessness in budgetary matters.

[45] Letter of Fazlı Tung.

interested the famous Marshal Ahmet Muhtar Pasha, who served as the Sultan's High Commissioner in Egypt from 1885 to 1906, in the cause, and every issue of *Mizan* finding its way into the country was feverishly scanned for the expected news that the renowned "Opener of Breaches" was advancing on Constantinople from Syria at the head of the 5th Army.[46]

Of the two publications of the society which were now trickling into Turkey from abroad through the foreign post offices, *Mizan* was by far the more popular. Ahmet Riza and *Mechveret* were held in ill repute, for Riza's intransigent attitude was more adapted to losing friends than to making them. His insistence on using *"Intizam ve Terakki"* ("Order and Progress") instead of *"Ittihat ve Terakki"* ("Union and Progress") coupled with his other Positivist manifestations and activities led to the very real danger that the society would be accused of atheism. Such an accusation could have been a terrible weapon in the hands of Abdul Hamid, the Sultan-Caliph. It is true that Ahmet Riza was finally brought to realize the seriousness of this matter, for the Positivist motto was dropped after the thirty-second issue of *Mechveret*.[47] However, despite the fact that much of the material for *Mechveret* was sent from Constantinople, Ahmet Riza, when he felt so inclined, continued to ignore the directives of the society or to subordinate them to his own views.

Both of these characteristics of Ahmet Riza, his Positivist leanings and his overbearing ways, kept the Young Turks in exile in a constant uproar. Arif Bey Oğlu, one of the Young Turks of Geneva, wrote to Ibrahim Temo on June 27, 1896 to express his concern about the use of the Positivist calendar on *Mechveret's* masthead. "What I am afraid of," he wrote, "is that if Istanbul publishes this among the already uneducated

[46] *idem.* Actually it would appear that Ahmet Muhtar simply led on the Young Turks who sought refuge in Egypt, and kept Abdul Hamid informed. See Martin Hartmann, *Unpolitische Briefe aus der Türkei*, vol. III of *Der Islamische Orient: Berichte und Forschungen* (Leipzig, 1905-1910), p. 135.

[47] Fesch, *op. cit.*, p. 337. The motto was restored with the issue of December 1, 1898, but met no opposition since Ahmet Riza was then fighting Abdul Hamid virtually single-handed.

public, the little sympathy which exists in our favor will be ruined, and we will not be able to accomplish anything after this." Moreover, he remarked, "If we had enjoyed conforming to the will of one person, then we would have conformed to the will of a 600-year-old dynasty. Since we have refused to accept their rule, why should we conform to the will of Ahmet Riza?"[48]

While the Turks in exile were wrangling thus, the plot to dethrone Abdul Hamid was gaining momentum in Constantinople, possibly without the knowledge of the Paris and Geneva branches.

Haji Ahmet Efendi appears to have become president of the central committee of the society in Constantinople in 1896. Under his general guidance were various other groups, including one under Sheyh Naili which was composed chiefly of *ulema*—the learned men of Islam—and magistrates, and one at the War Office under Lieutenant Colonel Shefik Bey. Presumably by this time the various students' committees had also accepted Haji Ahmet's leadership.[49]

The society's planned coup d'état was scheduled to take place in August 1896. Why this particular date was chosen cannot be stated definitely, although one reason is more or less obvious. The organization had been in existence for some years with the avowed purpose of overthrowing the ruling Sultan and presumably planned to strike as soon as it was able to do so. The society had been impeded by arrests from time to time, but it now had a large enough membership in Constantinople to

[48] Ibrahim Temo, *İttihad ve Terakki*, pp. 81-84. The same letter may also be found in Kuran, *İnkılâp Tarihimiz ve İttihad ve Terakki*, pp. 67-68. Fazlı Tung comments on the same thing in the following words: "Ahmet Riza Bey, after commencing work, made use of his title in a very skillful manner, conceiving of himself as a 'he shall not be asked of his doings' representative." The phrase is Koranic (Sura XXI) and refers to God, the implication being that Ahmet Riza had a somewhat exalted view of his powers. Tung quotes the phrase in Turkicized Arabic: "layüs 'el ama yef 'el."

[49] Here I am following Fesch, *op. cit.*, p. 331, as my Turkish sources are not very precise in this particular matter. It may be that the organization outside of the schools had become more or less independent after getting its start from the students' committees.

achieve its goal. However, a certain impetus was almost un-doubtedly given by the Armenian question, which reached its climax in that same month, August 1896.

The inference should not be drawn from the above that the Young Turks of 1896 sympathized with the aspirations of the Armenian revolutionary societies any more than did the Young Turks of 1908. For one thing it seems to be axiomatic that na-tionalists have no sympathy with the parallel desires of other nationalities; for another, the Committee of Union and Prog-ress was, paradoxically enough, inclined to side with the Sultan against any attempt to dismember the Ottoman patrimony. There were, of course, individuals who were horrified at the excesses of Abdul Hamid, but by and large what the Armenian question meant to 'most of them was that their country was attracting far too much unfavorable attention from the European powers and that interference in the affairs of the Ottoman Em-pire might well be imminent.[50] A concrete manifestation of this possibility was the international commission which sat during the spring and summer of 1896 to study the Armenian problem and suggest reforms. In the same way the fear that Abdul Hamid was losing Crete must also have acted as a stimulus.

To further their designs, the conspirators enlisted the aid of Kâzım Pasha, commandant of the 1st Division in Constanti-nople. Kâzım was won over by Haji Ahmet, and the execution of the coup was placed in his hands. The plan apparently was to occupy the Sublime Porte during a session of the Council of Ministers and simultaneously to seize Reshat Efendi, the heir apparent to the throne. A *fetva* would then be obtained from the *Sheyhülislam*[51] authorizing the deposition of Abdul Hamid

[50] Just how imminent this interference was the conspirators never knew. Actually Abdul Hamid came very close to being deposed by the powers in 1896. Even the German Emperor temporarily forsook the Sultan when he heard the news of the Constantinople massacres of 1896, and it would appear that had any one power taken the initiative, the others would have concurred and taken part in the partition of the Ottoman Empire. See William L. Langer, *The Diplomacy of Imperialism*, vol. 1, chap. x.

[51] *Fetva* is defined in Sir James W. Redhouse, *A Turkish and English Lexicon* (new impression, Constantinople, 1921), p. 1365, as "An opinion or

and his replacement by the previously deposed Murat V, or, if Murat proved to be incapable of assuming the responsibility, by the next in line of succession, Abdul Hamid's brother Reshat.[52]

Considering that the conspiracy was by this time so widespread and embraced so many highly-placed persons, it might well have accomplished its aims had not the projected coup d'état been discovered before it was able to materialize. And, inasmuch as any change in the government of the Ottoman Empire in 1896 could only have been for the better, the historian can only observe with regret that the plot was uncovered on the very eve of what was to have been its dénouement.

The existence of the conspiracy was actually revealed accidentally in an episode which is reminiscent of a musical comedy sequence, although the results were far from comic for the participants. Nadir Bey, director of a school known as *Nümunei-terakki* (literally "Example of Progress") and a member of the

---

decision as to a requirement of canon law, formally given by an officer duly appointed for the purpose of giving such opinions." The successive depositions of Abdul Aziz and Murat V in 1876 were both sanctioned by *fetvas* of the *Sheyhülislam*, whose position in the Ottoman Empire was roughly that of Minister of Canon Law. The fact that the Ottoman Empire was a theocratic state and that the Ottoman Sultans were the recognized spiritual leaders of a good portion of the Mohammedan world made this sanction of *fetva* of great importance. It is quite likely that, had the coup d'état been successful, the *Sheyhülislam* would have been able to discover sufficient reasons under canon law to authorize the deposition of Abdul Hamid, for Moslem canon law is much like any other in that a suitable answer for almost anything can be found in it if necessary. It is even possible that the *Sheyhülislam* was in on the conspiracy, particularly in view of the fact that so many of the *ulema* class were members of the society.

[52] Fesch, *op. cit.*, pp. 332ff.; letter of Fazlı Tung. Ahmed Bedevi Kuran, *İnkılâp Tarihimiz ve İttihad ve Terakki*, p. 65, states that Reshat was also in on the plot, having been won over by the *sheyh* (i.e. head) of the Mevlevi Dervish chapter in Constantinople's Beyoğlu quarter. Reshat, it seems, was a member of the Mevlevi order. (See below, chap. IV, for a discussion of the role of the Dervish orders in the Young Turk movement.) With respect to Murat V, who had been deposed in 1876 on the grounds of insanity, there was a strong suspicion that this was merely a device of Abdul Hamid to obtain the throne. This suspicion was enhanced by the fact that Murat had been held in complete isolation since 1876. One abortive attempt had already been made to free Murat—the ill-fated enterprise of Ali Suavi in 1878.

society, repaired to Tokatliyan's restaurant in Constantinople to indulge in a premature celebration of the events which were to take place on the following day. There he encountered one Mazhar Bey, a teacher in his school, and Mazhar's father Zülflü[53] Ismail Pasha, who was inspector general of the military schools. Nadir Bey had evidently exceeded his capacity for alcohol, for his first remark to the Pasha was, "*Paşam bilsen yarın neler olacak*," which may be translated as, "If the Pasha only knew what is going to happen tomorrow." Ismail Pasha's curiosity being aroused, he persuaded Nadir Bey to divulge the whole story by feigning sympathy with his views (and probably by keeping his glass filled). With the information he acquired, Ismail Pasha went immediately to the palace, and during the night all the participants in the plot were rounded up.[54]

For the conspirators the result was exile to remote parts of the empire. The list of exiles included all the ringleaders: Kâzım Pasha, Haji Ahmet, Sheyh Naili, together with his brothers Hakki Bey and Ayni Bey and eighteen other members of his family, Sheyh Abdülkadir[55] and twenty members of his family, Mekkeli Sabri, Zühdü Bey, Chief of the Bureau of Accounts of the Ministry of Finance (*Divani Muhasebat Reisi*), Kemal Bey, Public Prosecutor of the Council of State (*Şurayı Devlet Müddei-umumisi*), and numerous others.[56] All were

[53] "Zülflü" means "having side locks of hair." Ismail Pasha had side-whiskers, common enough in Turkey at that time, and was called "zülflü" to distinguish him from others having the name Ismail. See footnote 4, above.

[54] The above account is from the letter of Fazlı Tung. Fesch, *op. cit.*, has virtually the same story except that in his version Nadir Bey tried to convert Mazhar Bey to the views of the society in front of Ismail Pasha and was finally so carried away by his enthusiasm and what he had had to drink that he cried, "Mom cher ami, combien je regrette votre obstination. Demain il sera trop tard, et malheur à ceux qui ne seront pas avec nous!" Dr. Akil Muhtar Özden is not as easy on Nadir; in his letter he states bluntly that the plan miscarried because of Nadir's *treason*.

[55] Sheyh Abdülkadir outlived Abdul Hamid only to be hanged as a traitor by the Kemalist government for his connection with the Kurdish revolt of Sheyh Sait in the Diyarbakır area in 1925.

[56] Letter of Fazlı Tung; see also Fesch, *op. cit.*, p. 334, as well as the letters of Dr. Akil Muhtar Özden and Fehmi Janer.

herded aboard a ship and distributed to the places appointed for their exile. Those considered the most dangerous were put down in Libya. Thus Sheyh Naili and his relatives were settled in such places as Homs and Bengazi, while Haji Ahmet was forced to take up his residence in Fezzan. Mekkeli Sabri was sent to Mosul, but after some years was able to escape and find his way to Paris.[57] Lieutenant Colonel Shefik Bey went to Acre, but escaped almost immediately to Paris, where he became one of the leaders in the party.

As for Kâzım Pasha, he was sent off in disgrace to become governor of Scutari in Albania, a lenient punishment for a soldier known to have been seeking the overthrow of his sovereign.[58] The lesser conspirators were scattered about the southern and eastern vilayets of the empire and the coast of Anatolia.

It is difficult to perceive the logic in Abdul Hamid's policy of exiling. Legally speaking, all of the conspirators of 1896 were guilty of treason, and it should not have been too difficult for so ruthless a man as Abdul Hamid to procure their execution. It may be, of course, that he felt that the Armenian massacres had already attracted too much attention, but he followed the same policy throughout his reign. Many of those sent into exile made good their escape, as we have seen, and countless others lived to spread their ideas throughout the land. Thus the Sultan, while cutting out the most dangerous single spot of infection in his domains, was at the same time spreading the disease over a much larger area. Some of the exiles did die in their out-of-the-way spots, and a few, such as Midhat Pasha at an earlier date, were deliberately murdered while in exile, but by and large the Sultan's policy—or lack of policy— must be regarded as one of the factors which helped to bring about his downfall.[59]

[57] *idem.*

[58] Fesch, *loc. cit.* He subsequently was appointed director of construction for the Hejaz railway, begun by Abdul Hamid in 1900 in an effort to win the approval of the Moslem world. The railway made the pilgrimage to Mecca considerably easier.

[59] Cf. the case of Ziya Gökalp in Diyarbakır in 1906 and 1907 (Uriel Heyd, *Foundations of Turkish Nationalism* [London, 1950], p. 30).

Nadir Bey, whether dupe or rogue, was not treated in the same fashion as the others. According to Fesch, he was rewarded and decorated by the Sultan and lived bowed down with shame and remorse, unable to refuse the honors he did not desire.[60]

In Constantinople, the society was, of course, severely shaken by the arrest and exile of its leaders, but there was still no thought of abandoning the work. For a time there could be no serious activity, inasmuch as the palace was now thoroughly aroused and the Sultan's spies doubly vigilant, so that it would have been foolish to attempt anything until the excitement died down.

Nevertheless, the society was far from dead. The Young Turk publications, particularly *Mizan*, were still finding their way into the country, and the Young Turks inside the empire took heart from the words of Murat Bey, who had become for them the real leader of the movement. Haji Ahmet and his colleagues were gone, but they had gone as brave men, and the mantle had now fallen on the shoulders of Murat. So, although friends dared not stop to pass the time of day on the streets of Constantinople for fear the Sultan's spies would denounce them, the members of the society took courage from the fact that the work was being carried on outside the empire. *Mizan* was passed from hand to hand, and revolutionary notices began to appear on the main streets and on the doors of the mosques.[61]

In the fall of 1896 most of the remaining Young Turk leaders were in Europe, where they concentrated chiefly in Paris and in Geneva. From these vantage points they kept up a steady hail of vituperation which caused Abdul Hamid to seethe with anger. He was already very sensitive about *Mechveret*, which he had fought bitterly since its establishment and was still fighting. Shortly after Riza had commenced his barrage, the Sultan had persuaded the French government, then headed by

[60] Fesch, *loc. cit.*; Fazlı Tung states that Nadir was exiled, however, but only to Konya in Anatolia. Dr. Adnan Adıvar told the author that Nadir was not exiled but given charge of the school for Turkey's nomadic tribesmen in Constantinople.

[61] Letter of Fehmi Janer.

Léon Bourgeois, to suppress *Mechveret* and expel its director from France. Nothing daunted, Riza set up shop in Switzerland, while the French press, unanimous for once, took up the cudgel for freedom of the press and, incidentally, for the right of the Young Turks to say what they pleased. Clemenceau and others were in the forefront of those who were vociferously demanding the reversal of the decision, and in the face of all this pressure, the government gave way and raised its interdiction of everything except "the circulation in France of the Journal *Mechveret,* published in Paris in the Turkish language."[62]

Furious, the Sultan pursued the paper to Switzerland and, unable to get at this thorn in his side in any other manner, purchased the type used to print *Mechveret.* Ahmet Riza countered by bringing the paper out in a lithographed edition and then moved it to Belgium. Meanwhile he brought great joy to the members of the society in the empire by publishing an eight-page supplement (April 15, 1896) containing nothing but articles from the French press supporting the Young Turks in their fight against the Sultan.

In July 1897 the Sultan renewed the attack on Ahmet Riza and his colleagues by causing the Turkish Embassy in Paris to bring suit against the editors of *Mechveret* for defamation of character. The defendants were brought before the 9th Chamber of the Seine, and on August 15 the court, after hearing a deposition made by Clemenceau, handed down a judgment which, although in favor of the plaintiff, was like a slap in the face to the Sultan. The decision was embodied in the following words:

The tribunal,

Whereas Houillon, in his capacity as responsible editor of the journal *Mechveret,* for at least three months has published in Paris articles made the object of the order of the instructing magistrate;

[62] *Journal officiel,* April 12, 1896, as quoted by Fesch, *op. cit.,* p. 336; Karl Blind, "Young Turkey," *Fortnightly Review,* LXVI (December, 1896), pp. 835-836, notes that the Turkish edition was banned because it was believed to be more strongly worded than the French, a charge which was denied by Riza.

Whereas these articles contain offenses against the person of the Sultan, who is styled "cheat, hangman, scourge of God, bloody majesty, bloody despot, degenerate tyrant, disgrace of the Mussulmans, wolf guarding the sheepfold, red Sultan, etc.";

Whereas Halil Ganem and Ahmed Riza Bey have in the same circumstances of time and place rendered themselves accessories to the misdemeanor specified above in remitting to Houillon for publication in the journal *Mechveret* these articles of which they are the authors;

But, whereas the recognized honorableness of the accused, the sentiments towards France of Ahmed Riza and of Halil Ganem, who has become a naturalized Frenchman, the emotion and the reprobation which were inspired in them by the massacres of Armenia and under the force of which they have written the incriminating articles, the violent campaign of the French press against the Sultan, the ardent discussions in the Chamber of Deputies on the occasion of the same events are of a nature to excuse the excesses of pen of the accused and to invoke all the indulgence of the tribunal;

For these reasons,

Sentences the accused each to 16 francs of amends;
Orders that the execution of the penalty be suspended, etc. (Loi Bérenger).[63]

Among the Young Turk leaders who were congregated in Geneva and Paris by the end of 1896 were Ishak Sükûti, Sherefeddin Magmumî, Selânikli Nazim, Tunali Hilmi, Ibrahim Temo, Midhat Shükrü, Ali Zühdü, Chürüksulu Ahmet, and a number of others. Late in 1896 the Egyptian government began to manifest uneasiness about Young Turk activity, and Murat Bey was ordered by the directing committee of the society to transfer his operations to Europe.[64] There he immediately became the leader of the anti-Riza faction within the society and succeeded in attracting most of the members to his side.

Some mention has already been made of Ahmet Riza's unpopularity with his colleagues. Actually his attitude toward most of the fundamental aims of the society was the same as

[63] Quoted in *Revue Occidentale*, sec. sér. xv (September, 1897), pp. 216-217.
[64] Fesch, *op. cit.*, p. 338; Stern, *Jungtürken and Verschwörer*, p. 221. See also below, pp. 50ff., for an account of the circumstances of his departure.

that of most of the other Young Turks. In one important respect he differed sharply with the others, however: he was an evolutionist rather than a revolutionist. That is to say, Riza was at one with his co-workers in desiring to see Abdul Hamid pass out of the picture, in wanting to "Ottomanize" the population of the Turkish Empire, and in demanding the restitution of the Turkish constitution of 1876, but he refused to sanction the use of violence to achieve these ends because of his utter devotion to Positivist doctrines, which emphasized orderly progress. Thus his adherence to the Comtist "party line" coupled with his refusal to take orders from the committee brought about the estrangement.

Murat Bey, in contrast to Ahmet Riza, was extremely popular, and his literary efforts had already given him a considerable following in the society. In his favor also was the fact that he was a Pan-Islamist. His highest ambition was to see all Moslems rescued from foreign domination through the Caliphate and then to see this work crowned by the establishment of a great Islamic Empire.[65] He dreamed constantly of setting the feet of the Padishah on the path to this goal. While many of the Young Turks prided themselves on being freethinkers, they could not help being fired by Murat's ardent talk, if for no other reason than that the hegemony in any such empire as that envisaged by Murat would fall naturally to the Turks by virtue of the fact that the Ottoman Sultans were also the most widely recognized claimants to the position of Caliph. Thus his program offered an appeal on nationalist as well as on religious grounds.

As a result of all these factors Murat became the lion of the society and was, shortly after his arrival from Egypt, elected president of the Geneva branch[66] of the Committee of Union and Progress. Second in command was Chürüksulu Ahmet. *Mizan* and *Mechveret* were both continued as organs of the society, the former in Geneva and the latter in Paris. Both were

[65] Letter of Fazlı Tung.

[66] There was a constant coming and going between Geneva and Paris, so that, although the headquarters was officially in Geneva, there was almost as much activity in Paris.

at least theoretically under the control of the committee in Constantinople, and in addition all articles were subject to the scrutiny of the European subcommittee, on which Ahmet Riza was now subordinated to Murat.

Shortly after Murat's arrival in Europe the Khedive paid a visit to Paris. He was accompanied by Dr. Ismail Ibrahim, leader of the Young Turks in Egypt. According to Ismail Ibrahim, who probably had been associated with the society in its infancy at the Military Medical School in Constantinople, the Khedive was very sympathetic to the Young Turk movement at this juncture.[67] He was reluctant, however, to espouse the cause openly, and insisted on dealing with Ahmet Riza and Murat only through Ismail Ibrahim.

It did not take the Khedive long to conceive a dislike for Ahmet Riza, whose Positivism he viewed with distaste. But it was Murat who managed to estrange him completely by taking violent offense when the Khedive refused to receive him in his hotel suite. The upshot was that Abbas Hilmi washed his hands of the whole movement and even permitted the Sultan's agents to undermine the remnants of the society in Egypt. Ismail Ibrahim himself quit the society in disgust as a result of Murat's behavior.[68]

[67] Letter from Dr. Ismail Ibrahim to Temo dated January 27, 1897; in Temo, *op. cit.*, pp. 96-105; also reproduced in Kuran, *İnkılâp Tarihimiz ve İttihad ve Terakki*, pp. 77-82.

[68] *idem*. Ismail Ibrahim's letter is long and impassioned; he was obviously beside himself with rage and despair. Temo prints the letter without comment, but Kuran states flatly that the Khedive was dealing with the Young Turks under orders from Abdul Hamid and that Ismail Ibrahim was being used as a tool. Nevertheless, in view of the Khedive's known dislike for the Sultan, there is room for the assumption that he was at least half sincere in his dealings with Ismail Ibrahim and through him with the society. If so, it could well have been Murat's idiotic behavior which pushed him into the other camp. From this time on the Khedive pursued a vacillating policy with respect to the Young Turks, sometimes affording them sanctuary and sometimes expelling them from Egypt. In 1900 he made at least a perfunctory attempt to persuade the Sultan's brother-in-law, Damat Mahmut Pasha, to return to Constantinople (see below, chap. III). In his memoirs, Abdul Hamid's chamberlain, Tahsin Pasha, renders a very harsh judgment on Abbas Hilmi, of whom he says, "Degeneracy to this degree is a really frightening thing." (*Abdülhamit ve Yıldız Hatıraları* [Istanbul, 1931], p. 109). Tahsin was, of course, a

In May 1897 the headquarters of the society was transferred from Constantinople to Geneva.[69] At the same time the quarrel between the two factions in the organization came to a head. On May 15 *Mechveret* carried the following notice: "The Committee of union and of progress has the honor of informing the readers of the *Mechveret* that its president, M. Mourad Bey, and its director, M. Ahmed Bey de Tchuruksou, are going to Geneva to pass the summer season. . ."[70] The next issue of the paper announced that Murat had resigned and that Ahmet Riza had been excluded from the Committee of Union and Progress.[71] Riza, however, was to continue to edit the Turkish edition of *Mechveret*, but with a council of surveillance to act as a board of censorship.

Ahmet Riza kept on with his work, for whatever his faults may have been, he was not one to abandon the struggle against Abdul Hamid. Nevertheless, he did not submit tamely to his degradation. In an interview published in *La Patrie* on July 4, 1897, he admitted that a schism had developed within the society and hinted that it was connected with his defense of the rights of non-Moslem inhabitants of the Ottoman Empire.[72] This drew an indignant reply in the columns of *Mizan*, and with some reason, for all of the Young Turks, regardless of faction, could claim to have advocated the restoration of the constitution of 1876 with its guaranty of the freedom of religious belief. This is not to say that they sympathized with the struggles for national expression of any of the minority groups in the empire, but then Riza's writings display exactly the same attitude in this respect.

In June 1897 Murat Bey published a booklet which provides

---

faithful servant of Abdul Hamid, and his judgment may not be completely unbiassed.

[69] Letter of Dr. Akil Muhtar Özden.

[70] Quoted by Fesch, *op. cit.*, p. 338.

[71] Presumably this meant that Riza was excluded from the directing committee rather than from the society as a whole. *Mizan* of June 21 went so far as to say that Riza wanted to make the Paris committee a dependency of the Positivist society. *idem*.

[72] *ibid.*, pp. 338-340.

us with a useful summary of Young Turk thought at this period.[73] The exiled Young Turks always felt a strong compulsion to explain to the rest of the world that the Turks were not the terrible ogres they were often made out to be in the popular conception. Consequently, Murat demonstrates in this booklet, to his own satisfaction at least, that all the evils of the Ottoman Empire can be traced to two main sources: Abdul Hamid, of whom he says, "Ce n'est plus un Sultan, mais Satan qui règne!"[74] and the great powers. Vigorously denied is the allegation that the Moslem faith is responsible for the condition of the empire; thus one of his chapters is headed: "Islam is fundamentally liberal; fanaticism is not a natural consequence of Islam."

Typically Young Turk is the following analysis of the minorities problem:

The question of the Christians of Turkey is not a fruit ripened on the soil of the Ottoman Empire; this question had its birth in the diplomatic chancelleries.

Strange coincidence! the Christians of the Orient commence to suffer from the time of this ingenious and *humanitarian* invention![75]

A great deal of space is given by Murat to the Armenian situation, and again his attitude is indubitably that of the society in general. After first dismissing as "unpardonable" the presence of the "pretended" Armenian delegates at the Congress of Berlin, Murat declares sweepingly,

Assuredly, a special Armenian question, outside of the question of general reforms in Turkey, *must not and cannot be raised,* for the excellent reason that not a single basis whatsoever exists for the erection, even artificial, of an Armenia.[76]

Murat then points out that his offer to cooperate with the Armenians "for the good of the common fatherland" has been refused by the recognized Armenian committees and that

[73] Mourad-Bey, *La Force et la Faiblesse de la Turquie: Les Coupables et les Innocents* (Geneva, 1897), 59 pp.

[74] *ibid.,* p. 45. This blast against Abdul Hamid is of particular interest in view of the fact that Murat tamely submitted to this same "Satan" less than two months later.

[75] Mourad-Bey, *op. cit.,* p. 27. The italics are Murat's.

[76] *ibid.,* pp. 45-46.

. . . by this same refusal, they demonstrate that their aspirations are entirely apart from the welfare of Turkey, that is to say of this common fatherland of today and—infallibly—of tomorrow also. They wish, with true naiveness, to cause a new Armenia to arise from the debris of the present Ottoman Empire. This idée fixe, this maladroit project, pushes them to criminal resolutions, exercises with the unique purpose of exciting the susceptibilities of the Moslems. But they are past masters in the practice of deceit, and their maladroit and impolite manners, which give rise to the expression: *Armenianism*, aid them admirably to this end.[77]

Such remarks as these can scarcely have been conducive to friendly relations with the Armenians, and, indeed, it was just such sentiments as those expressed by Murat which effectively barred any possibility of intercourse with the Armenian revolutionary societies throughout the fight which they waged separately against their common enemy, Abdul Hamid.

Murat brings his little book to an end by summarizing his views in the following paragraphs:

1. The Moslem religion is not the direct cause of the weakness of the Ottoman Empire; no more does it constitute an obstacle to its recovery.

2. The population is young, vigorous, temperate, devout; their crime is in their blind obedience to the infamous authorities; but as diverse circumstances render this obedience sacred, this cannot be held against them too much.

3. The reigning family is degraded by the debauches of the Seraglio, but it is not worn out (épuisée). A 'purification' in line with the program of the party of reforms will restore to it its qualities so admired formerly.

Its presence at the head of the Empire is necessary; without it Turkish power has no existence.

4. The governmental organism demands a radical transformation. The infamy of those who govern comes, in the first place, from their ignorance and, in the second place, from the policy of Abdul-Hamid. The personnel of the public offices constitute a caste apart. It will be necessary to proclaim its fall and to reform it by the path of cooperation.

[77] Mourad-Bey, *op. cit.*, p. 48.

5. The reconstituted government must have a solid constitutional support which will permit it to protect the laws against the arbitrary encroachments of the Palace. This support will be, moreover, the key to the solution of the Ottoman problem. There are, amongst the present personnel, enough honest and enlightened men capable of constituting a normal government. The Oriental flexibility may perform wonders, once it is established that *the government demands that one* be honest and zealous. . . .

6. Thanks to this support and to an at least relative freedom of the press, the existing evils will be combatted, normal life and respiration, confiscated today by the Palace, will be restored to this society; the Moslem world will be taught that obedience to the established authorities being a virtue, even a very great virtue, nevertheless scarcely constitutes a rule without exception.

7. The Turks are ripe for a constitutional regime. The proportional representation of the Constitution of Midhat is a happy inspiration.

8. Sultan Hamid reigning, the Ottoman world and Europe cannot hope to obtain from him anything but troubles, more troubles, always troubles.[78]

The sterility of Young Turk thought at this time is only too evident from the above. There is absolutely no recognition of the fundamental problems confronting the Ottoman Empire, no appreciation of the forces at work in the modern world. Abdul Hamid is singled out as the source of most of the evils rampant in the Empire, and the remedy proposed is simplicity itself: remove the Sultan (but not the dynasty) and restore the short-lived Constitution of Midhat Pasha. Islam is still to be the cornerstone of the state, and the dynasty is needed to maintain the unity of the Empire. The subject nationalities are told that they are betraying their "common fatherland" by striving to achieve a national identity of their own, and they are offered the bleak alternative of becoming "Ottomans," an alternative which implies nothing but a continuation of the system in force under Abdul Hamid.

This pattern of thought is a curious mixture of incipient

[78] Mourad-Bey, *op. cit.*, pp. 58-59.

nationalism, imperialism, and what may be described as religious imperialism. The beginnings of Turkish nationalism are evident in the resentment of the interference of the European powers and in the fear of losing territory, yet in their attitude towards the Armenians and other subject peoples, the Young Turks are basically imperialistic. Such a mixture of ideas is not without earlier historical precedent, an almost classic example having been set by the Magyars with their intense nationalism and their equally intense contempt for the other nationalities over whom they ruled. To complicate matters still further, the Turks added another element, Islam, which, when added to the other issues, made the problems of the Empire almost insuperable.

The line of thought represented in Murat's brochure should not cause much surprise, however. Turkey at that time was still reposing in a sort of medieval twilight and can hardly be expected to have produced overnight men who were capable of understanding at once the nature of the malady of the "Sick Man of Europe." Like many of their former subjects in the Balkans, these Young Turks cast about them and came to the conclusion that the most significant thing about the states of modern Europe was parliamentary government. The logical solution to their own problems, then, was limited constitutional monarchy, and it is hard to blame them for concluding, like their contemporaries, that all one had to do was to set up the framework and let the machinery take care of everything else.

One of the most striking conclusions which can be drawn from Murat's booklet is that nearly every word in it could have been written by Ahmet Riza, and, as a matter of fact, was, in one way or another.[79] That is to say, the ideas expressed by Murat conflict in no important particular with Riza's ideas as evidenced by his writings both at this time and later. The reasons for the schism in Young Turk ranks have already been dis-

[79] cf. Riza's book *Tolérance Musulmane* (Paris, 1897), in which he maintained, like Murat, that Islam is fundamentally tolerant and even that the Ottoman government was basically tolerant. I have not seen this book of Riza's, but its main ideas are given by Carra de Vaux, *Les Penseurs de l'Islam*, vol. 5, pp. 159-161.

cussed; it is only necessary to repeat here that the split was not brought about by any fundamental disagreement on the aims of the society.

While the Young Turks of Europe were engaged in internecine strife, the society within the Empire was recovering from the heavy blow it had been dealt when the projected coup misfired. There were still many ardent young men in the military schools who were as determined as ever to keep up the fight against Abdul Hamid's government. Thus several of the students at the *Harbiye*, including such men as Fazlı Tung, Mahir Sait, and Giritli Abdülhalim, banded together and wrote to Chürüksulu Ahmet Bey, who had been their teacher of French before he fled the country, to ask what they could do to aid in the cause. They succeeded in getting the letter out of the country by means of one of the foreign post offices and then impatiently awaited a reply.

Chürüksulu Ahmet replied after a short interval, and, after praising the eager young men for their patriotism and determination, he authorized them, on behalf of the Committee of Union and Progress, to form a branch to be known as the "Süleyman Pasha Committee" in memory of an earlier patriot. He also acquainted them with the existence of another group, the "Hüseyin Avni Committee," in the class above them at the Military Academy, and urged them to work for the common cause with this group.[80]

In some of the other schools as well the organization was being kept alive. The Military Medical School was still providing the society with enthusiastic members despite all its setbacks, and there was also activity in the Artillery School.[81]

But the very eagerness of Mahir Sait, Fazlı Tung, and their colleagues helped to precipitate another wave of arrests. Some of the members of the new committee founded as a result of

[80] This account is based on the letter of Fazlı Tung. See also, Fesch, *op. cit.*, p. 341. Hüseyin Avni Pasha was Minister of War under Abdul Aziz, and Süleyman Pasha was Commandant of the Military Academy (*Harbiye*) at the same time. Both men were instrumental in the deposition of Abdul Aziz.
[81] Letter of Nahit Kervan.

the correspondence with Europe had been worried by the fact that certain passages of Chürüksulu Ahmet's letter had been so smudged as to be illegible, but the others had been too eager to pay any attention to the matter and had kept up the correspondence. Shortly thereafter the group was apprehended and imprisoned at Tashkishla,[82] the grim barracks where the permanent court-martial sat and worked at its backlog of unfortunate victims. There they spent dreary months awaiting their turn and discovered in the meantime that the man who had acted as their messenger to the foreign post office (they themselves dared not be seen in the post offices as the Sultan's spies kept constant watch on the people who went in and out), a commission merchant named Petro, had been conducting a profitable business by taking their letters to the government for copying before he posted them or brought them to the members of the committee.[83]

Severe measures were taken to stamp out the disaffection in the schools at this time. Two classes were taken out of the *Harbiye* at the same time, and the Military Medical School was removed to Haydarpasha across the Bosphorus.[84] But still the society was not smashed. It seemed to be indestructible, for it weathered blow after blow and then closed its ranks with grim determination and commenced anew to build up its strength for the moment when it could strike out at Abdul Hamid.

But while the remnants of the organization were engaged in licking their wounds after this last encounter, the most devastating blow of all fell without warning: the Young Turks of Europe, with one or two notable exceptions, suddenly gave up the struggle against Abdul Hamid. Some of them, led by the idol of the society, Murat Bey, even trooped back to the shores of the Bosphorus to kiss the feet of the man for whom their vocabularies of vilification had only the day before been stretched to the utmost. From this unbelievable stroke the society in Constantinople never recovered; never again during the reign of

[82] Now happily converted into a part of Istanbul Technical University.
[83] Letter of Fazlı Tung.   [84] Letter of Nahit Kervan.

46

Abdul Hamid did men gain courage enough to band together in that city; and in the whole of the Ottoman Empire opposition to Abdul Hamid by Turks was stilled for some years to come. The men who sat in Tashkishla were told the news and shown the triumphant announcement in the newspapers, and they could only bow their heads in shame for their former comrades and go to their exile with broken spirits.[85]

Most of the credit, if one may use the word in such circumstances, for bringing about the collapse of the Young Turk movement in 1897 must go to Ahmet Jelâleddin Pasha, a Circassian in whom the Sultan reposed especial confidence and to whom gossip had long assigned the unofficial title "Chief Spy of the Sultan."[86] Abdul Hamid had already made every effort to stifle the Young Turks living abroad. As we have seen, he worked through official channels when it suited his purpose and when he knew that circumstances would cause a foreign government to lend a favorable ear; Munir Bey, later Pasha, his ambassador in Paris, was forever being ordered to harass the Sultan's opponents in this fashion. There is also evidence that some of the Sultan's spies wormed their way into the Committee of Union and Progress for the purpose of bringing about dissension. But not until Ahmet Jelâleddin Pasha was dispatched to Europe were any lasting results obtained.

The split between Murat and Ahmet Riza had, of course, considerably aided the Sultan, and it undoubtedly facilitated Jelâleddin Pasha's task. But somehow Jelâleddin discovered that Murat Bey, despite his bitter attacks on the Sultan, was the weakest link in the chain as well as the most important and that it was quite likely that if Murat succumbed his disciples would follow suit.

It is true that the society laid down its arms—its publications —only after securing assurances from Jelâleddin Pasha that

---

[85] Some 81 Young Turks were tried by court-martial in June, 1897. Of these, 13 were condemned to death, but their sentences were subsequently commuted to imprisonment in the fortress in Tripoli, a fate which was hardly better.

[86] Fesch, *op. cit.*, p. 78.

the Sultan would make concessions and introduce reforms. The whole arrangement was referred to as a "truce," and the Young Turks reserved the right to resume the fight in the event that their conditions were not met. It is also probably true that most of the men who consented to the truce were perfectly sincere in their belief that they were doing the right thing, but they must nevertheless bear the blame for a fundamental error in judgment which set their cause back for a number of years. Conversely, full credit must be given to such men as Ahmet Riza and Halil Ganem, for whatever their faults, they at least were wise enough to realize that promises from Abdul Hamid meant nothing.

Ahmet Jelâleddin Pasha exercised some subtlety in the arguments he used with Murat Bey. He pointed out that the Sultan had a great sense of pride and that the Young Turks could never hope to achieve their aims on the tack they were following. He was able to convince Murat that the Sultan had finally realized that he must grant reforms but, because of his position, could not do so if it appeared that he was being forced into it. This seemed logical enough to Murat, and Jelâleddin followed up his advantage by adopting the confidential tone of one who is so anxious to help that he exceeds his instructions. Thus he suggested to Murat that anything was possible if he played his cards carefully and, instead of insulting the Sultan, started flattering him and catering to his vanity and self-esteem.[87] He topped off his persuasive arguments with a concrete guarantee that a complete amnesty for all political prisoners and exiles would be granted if the Young Turks abandoned their campaign against the Sultan. The alternative would be an even more savage persecution of the members of the society.

There were, apparently, other influences at work on Murat as well. Perhaps the most important of these was his dream of an Islamic Empire. Jelâleddin Pasha may have played on this theme, but it was obvious in any case to Murat that he could do nothing to realize this ambition until he could get close to

[87] For this information I am indebted to Fazlı Tung.

48

the Sultan. Another thing which tortured him was the knowledge that his paper, *Mizan*, was helping to bring imprisonment and exile to many people within the Ottoman Empire. Particularly after the last wave of arrests, Murat seems to have felt that the game was hardly worth the candle, that the movement was not gaining enough ground to offset the misery they were producing. To cap it off, Murat's longing to see his children in Constantinople was making him completely neurasthenic.[88]

Many of Murat's colleagues argued with him and even threatened him in a vain attempt to make him change his mind, but he remained adamant and refused to abandon his stand even when the Constantinople committee ruled against it.[89] Although Jelâleddin Pasha was more than anxious to supply his wants, Murat refused to accept money from him, and borrowed enough from friends to purchase his ticket for Constantinople. After refusing to leave behind the publication rights to *Mizan*,[90] Murat took his departure for Turkey.

L'Eclair of August 7, 1897, reported the story in the following words:

Convinced that Abdul-Hamid is sincere when he threatens, the chiefs of the Young Turkish party have reflected gravely on their duty. And here is what they have decided.

The party will consent to a truce, but it will not disarm.

The members will flatly refuse all honors or personal compensations which are offered to them.

Mourad Bey, without accepting a single personal favor, will go alone to Constantinople as hostage. This is a new sacrifice on his

[88] *idem.* Fazlı Tung devotes a good deal of space to an analysis of these factors which influenced Murat's decision.

[89] Letter of Dr. Akil Muhtar Özden. The opinion of the branch of the Committee of Union and Progress headed by Ibrahim Temo in Rumania was also solicited. The reply from this group characterized the Sultan and his servants as the "bandits of Yildiz" and listed a number of conditions which they insisted must be inserted in any agreement "with people who do not keep their word." One of the conditions was that Ahmet Riza must be consulted. Temo and his associates also stated that unless these conditions were agreed upon by both sides, they would "absolutely disconnect" themselves from the society and continue the struggle. (Temo, *op. cit.*, pp. 146-151; Kuran, *op. cit.*, pp. 72-76.)

[90] Letter of Dr. Akil Muhtar Özden.

49

part, for in the event hostilities are resumed, he will undoubtedly pay for the movement with his life.

The Sultan will engage himself to grant, beyond the reforms, a gradual amnesty.

Ahmed Riza, the director of the *Mechveret*, although not possessing the confidence of all the party because of his Positivist and international ideas, will remain, on the field of battle, at the head of the struggle.[91]

Many attempts have been made since then to justify the action taken by Murat and his friends. Paul Fesch, for example, examines with sympathy the position in which the Young Turks found themselves.

What [he asks] do the Young Turks demand? Reforms, and liberty for the political exiles. They are granted all this: the Sultan gives his word of honor as Sovereign. To refuse would have been to create suspicion that their conduct concealed an arrière-pensée of personal interest. They had to accept.

On Abdul Hamid alone falls the shame of having forfeited honor![92]

Murat and the others may have come out of the whole sorry affair with their honor theoretically intact, but that is all they salvaged from the wreckage. They lost the esteem of their fellow countrymen and their own self-respect as well, and they gained the knowledge that they had lost all the groundwork of the past years. In return for this they had the empty consolation of knowing that a ruler who was without honor, a fact that they should have known anyway, had once more "forfeited" his honor. Some of these same individuals renewed the fight against Abdul Hamid when they realized what dupes they had been, but by that time irreparable damage had been done to their reputations and their cause.

As has been noted before, the main result of the truce of 1897 was to destroy almost entirely the organization of the society within the Empire and to set back the Young Turk cause for a number of years. Not until 1906 did the society commence to rebuild, or rather to build anew, inside of Turkey.

Fehmi Janer, who was himself a Young Turk, remarks that

[91] Quoted in Fesch, *op. cit.*, pp. 343-344.   [92] *ibid.*, pp. 344-345.

it is difficult as he looks back now to understand why the society in Constantinople took Murat's defection so hard.[93] There were other men of ability who could have taken the lead, but when the news of Murat's action reached Constantinople the whole structure simply collapsed like a house of cards in the wind.

The answer is probably to be found in the fact that the hopes of most of the men who dreamed of a new, revivified Ottoman Empire were centered in the person of Murat, the acknowledged leader and spokesman of the movement; when he suddenly turned out to be unworthy of the trust placed in him the shock was so profound that their minds were numbed, their faith shattered, and their spirits broken. With them there was no academic discussion of the preservation of honor. They simply felt that they had been betrayed and sold out by their leaders.

Actually, it is difficult to see how they could have felt otherwise, for Murat's submission was an almost incredible performance in view of his previous stand. It is, even today, not at all easy to look with anything but contempt on a man who could write one day that there was no hope for the Ottoman Empire as long as Abdul Hamid lived and then maintain the next day that he believed in the good faith of this same ruler.[94]

Murat's associates did nothing to ease the situation. Once they saw that he was not to be dissuaded, they shrugged their shoulders and made the best of it. Some simply stayed on in Europe to continue their studies, but others went so far as to accept appointments from the Sultan, although they were acute enough to take positions outside the country. Chürüksulu Ahmet, who held the rank of major in the Turkish Army, became the Turkish Military Attaché in Belgrade, a post which he held until the Revolution of 1908, and Shefik Bey, a lieutenant colonel, occupied a similar post in Vienna until his death some time later.[95]

The break was thus complete, both within and without the Empire, and Abdul Hamid could breathe easily once more.

[93] Letter of Fehmi Janer.
[94] For a strong indictment of Murat, see Edmond Fazy, *Les Turcs d'aujourd'hui ou la grand Karagheuz* (Paris, 1898), pp. 268-273.
[95] Fesch, *op. cit.*, p. 344.

CHAPTER III

The Young Turks in Exile—Ahmet Riza and Sabaheddin—The Congress of Ottoman Liberals—The Growing Cleavage Between the Factions

WITH THE ALMOST COMPLETE COLLAPSE of the Young Turk movement in the summer of 1897, Ahmet Riza and his associates found themselves virtually alone in maintaining the struggle against the Sultan. Throughout the negotiations with Ahmet Jelâleddin Pasha, *Mechveret* had bitterly resisted the move to compromise with Abdul Hamid, and its publishers had consequently been branded as intransigent by Murat and his colleagues.

The case for those who intended to continue the battle was stated by Halil Ganem in a letter to *L'Eclair* on August 9, 1897.

We are not intransigents, he wrote, but we do not believe in the promises of the Sultan; no more do we believe in his word, and we believe still less in the intermediaries he sends to us. We demand acts and deeds.

How is it that it is necessary for us to desist for him to inaugurate the reforms which he has promised a hundred times without ever deciding simply to make an honest effort?

May Mourad Bey forgive me! there was no need whatsoever for him to deliver himself as hostage to the Sultan. No one asked this sacrifice of him.

The program of our party is well known, and it will suffice that the Sultan incline towards this program for us to support and encourage him, for, although it causes us to abandon the struggle, we have it at heart to assure the present and guarantee the future of our country. Once more, promises are nothing, principles are everything.[1]

The logic of the position adopted by Riza and Ganem was irrefutable, and events bore them out completely, as has been seen.

---

[1] This letter was written in response to an article which had appeared two days earlier explaining why Murat Bey was giving up the fight; it is reproduced in Paul Fesch, *Constantinople aux derniers Jours d'Abdul Hamid*, p. 344; see above, Chap. II.

Two of the original founders of the Society of Union and Progress, Ishak Sükûti and Abdullah Jevdet (the latter had escaped from Tripoli and arrived in Europe just in time for the truce), soon decided that it had been a mistake to trust Abdul Hamid and founded in Geneva a new Young Turk organ, *Osmanli* (*Ottoman*). This paper soon achieved some prominence, and it began to appear as if *Mechveret* were to be relegated to its old position as the organ of the opposition within the movement, for other prominent Young Turks such as Tunali Hilmi, Nuri Ahmet, and Cherkes Mehmet Reshit soon associated themselves with the new journal.

Within a short time, however, the Sultan was able to dispose of this new threat to his peace of mind. Munir Bey, his ubiquitous ambassador and errand boy, approached Sükûti and Jevdet with a new compromise proposal. In return for the cessation of publication of *Osmanli*, the Sultan, Munir was empowered to state, would be willing to free the political prisoners in Tripoli and Fezzan. Abdullah Jevdet, who knew from firsthand experience what the conditions were in Tripoli, was naturally anxious to do what he could to alleviate the suffering of those who were still incarcerated in the grim fortress, and it is therefore not surprising to find that this proposal met with a favorable response. Early in 1899 *Osmanli* was suspended, and this time the Sultan carried out his part of the bargain—at least partially: the prisoners in Tripolitania were released from their formal imprisonment, but they remained there as exiles.[2]

Thus far one can sympathize with Sükûti, Jevdet, and the others who were associated with them in the publication of *Osmanli*, but they then proceeded to put themselves beyond the pale in exactly the same way as had Murat and his colleagues in 1897. In 1900 Ishak Sükûti accepted a position as "Medical Officer" to the Ottoman Embassy in Rome, and Abdullah Jevdet accepted a similar position with the Embassy in Vienna.

[2] Fesch, *Constantinople aux derniers Jours d'Abdul-Hamid*, p. 346.

Of the others, Tunali Hilmi became a Secretary at the Embassy in Madrid.[3]

Ishak Süküti did not abandon the cause altogether, for when Nuri Ahmet and Edhem Ruhi decided to go to England and continue publishing *Osmanli* in that country, Süküti underwrote the expenses of publication and continued to do so until his death in San Remo two years later.[4] Abdullah Jevdet later entered the lists against Abdul Hamid once more after becoming involved in an altercation with Mahmut Nedim Pasha, the Turkish ambassador in Vienna. However, Jevdet was never able to live down the fact that he had not only ceased fighting for the principles he had once maintained but had actually accepted a sinecure from the Sultan which amounted to little more than a thinly disguised bribe.[5] In any event, by the latter part of 1899, *Mechveret* was once again the only important champion of what now appeared more than ever to be a hopeless cause.[6]

At this juncture the attention of Europe was suddenly focussed on the Young Turk movement by a completely unexpected event. In December 1899 Damat Mahmut Pasha, the Sultan's brother-in-law,[7] fled the country with his two sons, the Princes Sabaheddin and Lutfullah. Damat Mahmut, born in 1855 to

---

[3] K. Süssheim, " 'Abd Allāh Djewdet," *Encyclopedia of Islam, Supplement* (1938), p. 56; Fesch, *op. cit.*, p. 346.

[4] Letter of Dr. Akil Muhtar Özden, dated May 4, 1941. *Osmanli* was subsequently underwritten by Prince Sabaheddin (see below) for a short time, but the paper finally disappeared in 1902 or 1903 after a precarious existence, first in London and then in Folkestone.

[5] "For twenty years he suffered unspeakably for it and only seemed to recover towards the end of his life. He never attained political office on account of his agreement with Abd ül-Hamid's agents." Süssheim, *loc. cit.*

[6] There were a number of other anti-Hamidian publications in circulation in various quarters, but none of them represented a very considerable group, and only *Mechveret* could trace its ancestry directly to the original society. Ibrahim Temo, the founder of the society, was publishing a Young Turk journal of sorts in Rumania, and there were one or two other papers in Egypt as well as in other places, but there was little or no coordination of their efforts.

[7] "Damat" is a Persian word which indicates, when used as a title, that the person so designated is the husband of a sister or aunt of the sovereign. It might be noted here that another Damat Mahmut Pasha, also a brother-in-law of the Sultan, was exiled and subsequently strangled with Midhat Pasha in 1884.

Admiral Halil Pasha and a daughter of Sultan Mahmut II, was a man of some intelligence and education. In his youth he had served for a time in the Embassy in Paris, and in 1892 he had occupied the Ministry of Justice for about eight months. He had repeatedly urged the Sultan to restore the Constitution of 1876, and, after meeting with no success in his endeavors, he had finally decided that his only alternative was to put himself outside the jurisdiction of Abdul Hamid and bring the full story of the Sultan's misrule to the attention of the outside world.[8]

It was immediately evident from the hue and cry set up by the Sultan that he had been touched in an extremely sensitive spot by the flight of his brother-in-law. All trains leaving the capital on the day that Damat Mahmut was discovered to be missing were delayed, and an entire regiment was called out to search the trains which had proceeded as far as Adrianople when the alarm was given.[9] A minor international incident was created when the only vessel to clear Constantinople that day was stopped and searched in the Dardanelles.[10]

Damat Mahmut had, however, anticipated the Sultan's reactions, and, by the simple expedient of remaining in hiding the first day and then by means of a small boat at night, boarding a French vessel which was already under way, he was able to slip through the dragnet undetected.[11] The ship carrying the royal fugitives passed through the Dardanelles unchallenged and deposited its passengers in Marseilles a few days later.

Meanwhile, Abdul Hamid was working frantically to discover some means of forcing his brother-in-law to return. Anticipating that Damat Mahmut would seek refuge in France, the Sultan

[8] I am depending here chiefly on Joseph Denais, *La Turquie Nouvelle et l'Ancien Régime* (Paris, 1909), pp. 43-44. Demetra Vaka, "An Imperial Enemy of Turkish Despotism," *Asia*, XXIV (January 1924), p. 36, maintains that Prince Sabaheddin, the elder son of Damat Mahmut, was responsible for persuading his father to flee.

[9] Fesch, *op. cit.*, p. 352.

[10] The Compagnie des Messageries Maritimes, which operated the vessel, obtained a large indemnity for this action; *ibid.*, p. 352.

[11] *ibid.*, pp. 351-352; Denais, *op. cit.*, p. 45.

instructed his representatives there to declare that Mahmut was really fleeing to escape the consequences of a series of crimes he had committed. These alleged crimes included the theft of his wife's jewels, the murder of a harem servant and the forcible abduction of his two minor sons, over whom he was said to have no jurisdiction inasmuch as they were the wards of the Sultan by Turkish law. To make the case even stronger, the Sultan further charged his representatives to report that Damat Mahmut had for some time before his flight showed signs of mental disorder.[12] The purpose of these maneuvers was to secure Damat Mahmut's extradition on criminal charges, for the Sultan was aware that no major European government would consider a political difference of opinion with one of the most cordially detested men in the world sufficient grounds for extradition.

Mechveret of January 1, 1900, reported the arrival in France of Damat Mahmut Pasha and his sons in the following words:

On the arrival of the steamer in Marseilles, the representatives of the press ascertained, not without astonishment, that Damad Mahmoud Pacha, represented as deranged by the official dispatch from Yildiz, is a gentleman of parts, not only sane, but even very enlightened and very liberal. They were able to perceive with no less stupefaction that the two minor children mentioned in the same dispatch are two gallant men, of whom the youngest is twenty-two years of age, completely emancipated not only from the ill-omened tutelage

[12] The Minister of Foreign Affairs in Constantinople sent the following dispatch to Turkish ambassadors and diplomatic agents in Europe: "Mahmoud Pacha Damad, qui donnait depuis quelques temps des signes de détraquement d'esprit, est parti sans autorisation en emmenant avec lui les deux fils mineurs de S. A. la Sultane son épouse. Comme, d'après nos lois, les fils du Sultan se trouvent sous la dépendance directe et absolue de Notre August Maître et comme, d'autre part, S. A. la Sultane réclame avec insistance ses deux enfants mineurs, je vous prie de faire effectuer immédiatement, par les moyens que vous jugerez les plus efficaces, des recherches minutieuses et, dans le cas où Mahmoud Pacha se trouverait ou arriverait dans le pays de votre résidence, de faire auprès des autorités compétentes des démarches pour qu'il soit immédiatement envoyé à Constantinople, sous surveillance, avec les deux enfants qu'il a enlevés sans en avoir aucun droit. D'ordre impérial, vous aurez à télégraphier sans retard le résultat de vos efforts." Fesch, *op. cit.*, p. 353, quoting *Mechveret* of January 1, 1900. An English version is to be found in Demetra Vaka, "Prince Sabaheddine as a Free-Lance Liberal," *Asia*, XXIV (February 1924), p. 120.

of their uncle Abdul-Hamid, but also from all sentiment of fanaticism and from reactionary prejudices.[13]

After the French government refused to comply with Abdul Hamid's demand for cooperation in returning his fugitive brother-in-law, Damat Mahmut was besieged by hordes of emissaries from the Sultan. Munir Bey, the Ottoman Ambassador in Paris, was an almost daily visitor for a time; the arch-mediator Ahmet Jelâleddin Pasha attempted to repeat the success he had had with Murat; and even the Khedive of Egypt dropped by to see what he could do on behalf of his suzerain.[14]

It was at first felt by the Sultan and his advisors that Damat Mahmut was simply playing the time-honored Turkish game of removing himself to a safe position before opening negotiations which would eventually culminate in a satisfactory financial settlement. One of the Sultan's envoys, possibly Ahmet Jelâleddin Pasha, remarked to the Swiss head of the tobacco administration in Constantinople that he was leaving for Paris and was confident that he had only to name the right price to succeed in bringing Damat Mahmut back.[15] However, as the various offers made by the Sultan continued to be firmly declined, it soon became evident that Damat Mahmut was in earnest.

One of Damat Mahmut's first acts on arriving in France was to address to Ahmet Riza a letter which was the ultimate in eulogy, as the following extract shows:

It is useless to express to you the profound recognition with which every Ottoman is imbued towards you for the very weighty services which you unremittingly render to the sacred cause of our country. You have all the more merit in that you have sacrificed your person

[13] Fesch, loc. cit.
[14] ibid., p. 359. The Khedive was en route to England in June 1900.
[15] Louis Rambert, Notes et Impressions de Turquie; l'Empire Ottoman sous Abdul-Hamid 1895-1905 (Geneva and Paris [1926]), p. 71, entry of January 26, 1900. Rambert notes further, "Le fait est que nous avons eu l'exemple de Mourad, l'ancien commissaire de la Dette publique, qui a joué le même jeu, et qui vit maintenant paisiblement dans sa propriété du Bosphore, surveillé sans doute par quelques espions, mais jouissant d'un traitement opulent." This is particularly interesting as evidence of the way in which Murat was regarded despite his and his apologists' explanations of the reasons for his return.

with the purpose of preparing a new life for the suffering Ottoman people. It is not given to everyone to remain, like you, firm and courageous in the midst of the innumerable difficulties which surround you.

To bring out the truth even more, I shall add that Turkey has not, perhaps, for a century seen a man such as you arise from her womb. If there were in Constantinople, and above all, near the Sultan, persons passionately devoted to justice and truth like you, I have no doubt whatsoever that most of the evils and calamities would never have assailed the Empire. . . .[16]

Ahmet Riza was not slow to respond. The party, he declared, was most happy to welcome a member of the royal family as an ally in the battle for the deliverance of the fatherland, and, he continued,

That which gives the most pleasure to my companions in the struggle and myself is that this testimonial of sympathy comes from a well-informed person, from a former minister, of broad and liberal ideas. His letter is a striking proof of the justice of our complaints against the ill-omened régime which is leading Turkey to ruin.

The prejudiced defenders of Abdul-Hamid will no longer be able to say that the partisans of reform are dreamers or embittered men. Who should know the Sultan better and from closer proximity than his brother-in-law? Who should be able to judge the political and social situation of the Empire with more competence than a former minister of Justice? It will be seen, in a few days, by a letter which he is addressing to the Sultan, what he thinks of that individual and his government.

We consider this courageous act of Mahmoud Pacha as a most happy event, not only for the party of Young Turkey, but for the people in its entirety; it will find an echo in the hearts of all those who are sworn to serve the sacred cause of the fatherland.[17]

The letter to which Ahmet Riza referred was addressed openly to Abdul Hamid by Damat Mahmut on January 21, 1900. It was a thoroughgoing indictment of the Hamidian re-

[16] Fesch, *op. cit.*, p. 354, quoting from *Mechveret* of January 1, 1900. Felice de Chaurand de St. Eustache, "L'Esercito nel Movimento Costituzionale della Turchia," *Revista d'Italia*, XI (October 1908), p. 524, states that Damat Mahmut had been making heavy financial contributions to Ahmet Riza before his flight, but I find no confirmation of this elsewhere.

[17] Fesch, *op. cit.*, p. 355.

gime in which the writer singled out for attention all the well-known faults of Abdul Hamid's government. The officials with whom the Sultan surrounded himself, he declared, were "igno-ramuses of low degree, debilitated oldsters or lying and corrupt intriguers," who prevented honest men from approaching their sovereign, and the miserable state of public instruction, finances, and the Navy were striking proof of the rottenness of the government. However, Damat Mahmut reserved his most scathing denunciations for the Sultan himself.

Damat Mahmut had one great advantage over European critics of Abdul Hamid: he was a Turk and a Moslem himself, as well as a member of the royal family. Because of these factors his field of attack was enlarged, and he could say things of the Sultan that no foreigner and no "Ottoman" of another religion could say without antagonizing the Turks in general. Thus, after pointing out that Abdul Hamid had a dual responsibility inasmuch as he was not only the Sultan of the Ottoman Empire but ex officio Caliph of the Moslem World as well, Damat Mahmut struck out at Abdul Hamid the Caliph as well as Abdul Hamid the Sultan.

Let me say to you then, in all frankness, Sire, that your administrative system does not resemble at all the fair and just government of a caliph, any more than it does that of the sovereigns of the European states. It has, rather, certain points of resemblance to that of certain tyrants who lived a few thousand years ago.[18]

None of Damat Mahmut's remarks was any more charitable, as the following extracts will bear witness:

As to Your Majesty, like certain despotic and egotistic monarchs, you take for the principle of your conduct and make yours the ill-starred saying of Louis XV: *Après moi, le déluge.* You think only of your own person, you trample on all rights and on all humanitarian sentiments. The welfare of the people is your last concern, and twenty-four million people are sacrificed to your egotism. . . .

You are the principal author of the ruin of our country and the cause of many basenesses and accumulated crimes. The blood which

18 Fesch, *op. cit.*, p. 356.

you have caused to be shed, the homes which you have destroyed, and the falsehoods which you have circulated dazzle all eyes.

In the past eight years I have submitted to you all these reflections many times. You have been able neither to appreciate the good intention nor to comprehend my devotion. Thus, certain that I would be unable to make you understand the truth as long as I was in Constantinople, I thought: inasmuch as the Sultan is incapable and refuses to listen and to understand, it is necessary that I enlighten the nation, that I expose to it the dangers of the present régime and the necessity of transforming it.[19]

A few months after Damat Mahmut's departure, Abdul Hamid was further infuriated by the flight of another prominent member of his entourage, Ismail Kemal Bey, an Albanian who had occupied a number of high positions in the Empire. Ismail Kemal, who also took his sons with him into exile, chose a simpler method of leaving the country than had Damat Mahmut; he simply put himself outside the jurisdiction of the Sultan by taking refuge aboard the *stationnaire* of the British Embassy.

Ismail Kemal tells us in his memoirs that his decision to leave Turkey was based on the fact that he was becoming an object of suspicion to the Sultan because of his constant attempts to secure reforms for the Empire, particularly through the medium of a bi-weekly newspaper which he published in Philippopolis.[20] Being a man of some intelligence, Ismail Kemal decided that it was time to leave when the Sultan appointed him Governor-General of Tripoli and made arrangements for him to sail for his new post immediately aboard the royal yacht. The chances of his reaching Tripoli, he felt, were small, so he put into effect the plan he had carefully prearranged with Sir Nicolas O'Conor, the British Ambassador, and went aboard the *stationnaire* lying in the Bosphorus. From here he was escorted to a vessel flying the British flag and sailed for Greece on May 1, 1900. "News of my departure having spread round Constantinople," writes

[19] Fesch, *op. cit.*, pp. 356-358; the letter is reproduced in its entirety by Fesch on pp. 355-358. A rather loose English version is given by Vaka, *op. cit.*, pp. 120-121.

[20] Sommerville Story (ed.), *The Memoirs of Ismail Kemal Bey* (London, 1920), pp. 277ff.

Ismail Kemal with no false modesty, "the quays were thronged by a vast concourse of the population, who had come to see me off and showed great sympathy with me."[21]

A European resident of Constantinople noted in his diary at this time,

> But it is truly singular to see these people escaping from the territory of a great Empire, absolutely like one breaks out of a penitentiary. There is a need of real subterfuge in order to succeed, and, when one has succeeded in passing the frontier everyone is beside himself and the Sultan himself manifests the same despair as a policeman who sees a prisoner flee whose guarding has been especially confided to him.[22]

Ismail Kemal, after sojourning for a time in Greece, went on to Western Europe and eventually took up his residence in Brussels. There he entered into an agreement with another Albanian, Faik Bey Konitza, to take over the management of a journal called *Albania* which Faik Bey had started in 1897. The two men did not get along, and after a short time Ismail Kemal started a new paper, *La Salut de l'Albanie*, published in Albanian, Turkish, and Greek.[23]

At this juncture Ismail Kemal was approached by the ubiquitous Munir Bey with an offer from the Sultan of the post of Ambassador-at-large, "with the mission of studying the different institutions of Europe and making reports on them so that they might serve as bases for reforms in Turkey."[24] This handsome offer was refused, and Ismail Kemal started off on a round of visits (an occupation of which he was very fond) to Albanians in Egypt and other places.

During the first year or two of the new century, as we have

[21] *ibid.*, p. 295; it might be noted that Ismail Kemal shows a certain tendency to overestimate his own importance in his memoirs. It is quite unlikely that any considerable group of people would have risked gathering at all, let alone to cheer one who had incurred Abdul Hamid's disfavor.

[22] Rambert, *op. cit.*, pp. 76-77. It is a sad commentary that what seemed astonishing to Rambert in 1900 now is commonplace in modern police states.

[23] Story, *op. cit.*, p. 303.

[24] *idem.*

seen, the Young Turk movement appeared to have taken on a fresh impetus and to have won back some of the ground lost in 1897. This was true, however, only of the movement outside of the Ottoman Empire, for there had been no attempt to reconstitute the internal organization of the first society in Constantinople.

The Young Turks abroad were nevertheless extremely articulate, especially after Damat Mahmut Pasha and his sons arrived in Europe, and theirs were not the only voices raised against Abdul Hamid. Of the minority groups of the Empire, there was scarcely a one which did not have its representatives in Paris—or Geneva or Brussels or London—and its own publications demanding either general reforms within the Empire or consideration of its own national interests.

Of the subject nationalities of the vast complex which made up the Ottoman Empire, the Armenians were the most vociferous, the best organized, and the ones who had attracted the greatest general sympathy throughout the world because of the persecution they had suffered. Thus, for example, in addition to the official publications of the Armenian revolutionary organizations such as the Hentchak and the Dashnagtzoutian, a fortnightly journal known as *Pro-Armenia* was founded in November 1900 by Georges Clemenceau, Anatole France, Jean Jaurès, Francis de Pressensé, and E. de Roberty to plead the Armenian cause.

It has already been noted that the Albanians were also active in Europe. Faik Bey Konitza and Dervish Hima had founded the journal *Albania*, to further the desires of certain elements for the autonomy of Albania within the framework of the Ottoman Empire. This paper was for some years after its inception strongly anti-Young Turk and pro-Abdul Hamid, for its directors—chiefly Faik Bey, as Dervish Hima dropped his connection with the publication after a time—seemed to have felt that they could achieve their aims more easily by taking this tack than by attacking the Sultan. It was probably for this reason that

Ismail Kemal Bey's arrangement with Faik Bey over *Albania* had disintegrated.[25]

In the first years of its publication, *Albania* devoted much space to crying that the Young Turks of Paris were "un groupe d'adolescents rusés et naifs" (which would seem somewhat paradoxical), composed chiefly of "jeunes dandys efféminés,"[26] and that the poor Sultan was merely the "victim" of the Young Turks, who were using him as a scapegoat for the people as a whole.[27] As late as 1901 Faik Bey was still adding to the already almost insuperable difficulties of bringing together the various anti-Hamidian factions with such ill-advised remarks as the following: "For myself, I can affirm that I have not yet encountered a SINGLE Turk who sincerely disapproves of the massacres of Armenia."[28]

For the Kurds, Abdürrahman Bederhan, son of a well known Kurdish chieftain who had resisted Turkish domination for years before submitting to Abdul Mejid in 1840, published the journal *Kurdistan* in London, and aided in the publication of *Osmanli*.[29] A number of Kurds, including Abdullah Jevdet and Ishak Sükûti, had been active in the Young Turk movement from the beginning, but they appear to have considered themselves Turks —or at least "Ottomans"—rather than Kurdish nationalists. By and large the concept of nationality developed later in the Moslem minorities than in the Christian.

As far as the Arabs were concerned, the only activity worthy of mention was carried on by an organization known as the "Turco-Syrian Reform Committee" under the leadership of Emir Emin Arslan. This organization had been in existence for

[25] Story, *op. cit.*, p. 303; Dervish Hima was, by 1901 or possibly earlier, publishing another Albanian journal, *Arnavutluk*, in Rome.

[26] *Albania*, I (April 1897), p. 27.

[27] *ibid.*, I (December 1897), pp. 130-131.

[28] *ibid.*, v (October 1901), p. 166.

[29] Bederhan participated in the Young Turk Congress of 1902 but by 1904 he had been prevailed upon by the Sultan's representatives to cease publishing his paper. In 1900 he had disowned his son, Osman Pasha, who was energetically putting down the Armenians in Turkey. Cf. *Pro-Armenia*, I (January 10, 1901), pp. 30-31.

some time, but again its adherents seem to have had no truly nationalistic impetus but rather a desire for reforms which would enable them to live within the Empire more easily. Halil Ganem, however, was a Christian Syrian, and his devotion to the Young Turk cause cannot be questioned, as we have seen above.

In the face of this welter of associations and journals and also because of the attitude of the various European governments, it is not surprising that the conviction arose amongst many of the Young Turks that every nationality in the sprawling Ottoman domains had its protector save for the Turks themselves. Thus we find Ahmet Riza complaining bitterly that no one takes the part of the poor Turk, who suffers as grievously from the iniquitous régime of Abdul Hamid as do any of the other inhabitants of the Sultan's realm—and, he points out,

> The consular agencies, the foreign schools, the houses of missionaries, covered by the capitulations, do not afford them a place of refuge, a magazine of arms, or a center of propaganda, as was the case with the Armenian and Bulgarian agitators. If the Turks are taken and condemned, the Tsar will not intervene in order to spare them; no more will they be conducted safe and sound aboard a vessel by the dragoman of the Russian Embassy if they introduce themselves into the Ottoman Bank.[30]

There was really a great deal of truth in what Ahmet Riza said, for, although the plight of the minorities, particularly the Christian minorities, in the Ottoman Empire was most unenviable under Abdul Hamid, the situation of the average Turk was not a happy one. As Sir Harry Luke says,

> Only the Turk himself evoked nobody's sympathy, despite the foreign interest extended to the Greeks, the Rumanians, the Bulgars, the Serbs, the Armenians. Perhaps it was partly his own fault, for he

[30] *Revue Occidentale*, sec. sér., XXVII (January 1903) p. 94; Riza is, of course, referring to the attempt by the Armenian Revolutionary Federation, the Dashnagtzoutian, to achieve its aims by seizing the Ottoman Bank in Constantinople in August 1896. See Langer, *Diplomacy of Imperialism*, I, pp. 322ff.

had not even begun to be interested in himself as one of his Padishah's oppressed or suppressed nationalities, while to outsiders he was identified with the defects and vices of his Government. Those critics of the Ottoman Government who in their charges against Turkish administration made the Turkish people the fellow-defendants of their rulers failed to realize how often the real Turks, that is to say, the Anatolian peasants, far from being identifiable with the Osmanli official, were regarded by the latter as merely the raw material of the State, almost as its helots, no more to be petted or protected than the least considered of *rayahs*. The Turkish section of the population had travelled far indeed from the early days of the Turkish advance into Europe, when the Turkish people constituted a nation in arms jointly reaping the benefit of their joint conquests.[31]

Despite the conflicts in ideologies and aspirations between the various factions, it was natural that some attempt would be made to coordinate the activities of the organizations which had one thing in common—the desire to overthrow the existing régime in the Ottoman Empire. The logical person to undertake such a task was Damat Mahmut Pasha, whose position put him, at least theoretically, somewhat above the squabbling of the others. Damat Mahmut was, however, suffering from an illness which was to result in his death early in 1903, and the leadership therefore devolved upon his sons, particularly Sabaheddin, a young man in his middle twenties who was beginning to develop some ideas of his own. Thus an "Appel Général aux Ottomans" went out from Egypt, where they were visiting, over the signatures of Sabaheddin and Lutfullah, calling on all "Ottomans" to meet in a Congress to discuss means of re-establishing liberty and justice in Turkey.[32]

The appeal was favorably received, and the first "Congress

[31] *The Making of Modern Turkey* (London, 1936), pp. 58-59. Luke is actually writing of the period just before the accession of Abdul Hamid, but his remarks apply equally as well to the period under consideration, with the exception that the Young Turks were finally beginning to realize that they were themselves one of the "Padishah's oppressed or suppressed nationalities."

[32] A long résumé of this appeal may be found in Fesch, *op. cit.*, pp. 365-367. The appeal was sent from Egypt because Damat Mahmut and his sons were constantly being forced to shift their residence at the request of the various governments who did not care to be embarrassed by harboring the royal fugitives.

of Ottoman Liberals" sat in Paris from the fourth to the ninth of February 1902. The meeting had at first been forbidden by the Ministry of the Interior at the request of Abdul Hamid, and plans were therefore made to assemble privately at the home of a French sympathizer, M. Lefèvre-Pontalis. The interdiction was subsequently withdrawn, but the first meeting was nevertheless held at Lefèvre-Pontalis' home, after which the Congress met at the home of Prince Sabaheddin.[33]

Some forty-seven delegates presented themselves at the Congress—Turks, Arabs, Greeks, Kurds, Albanians, Armenians, Circassians, Jews. The one—and the only—viewpoint which they shared in common was that Abdul Hamid left much to be desired in his capacity as Sultan of the Ottoman Empire, and the mistake that was made by Sabaheddin was in assuming that they felt any great bond in the fact that they all lived within the borders of this ramshackle empire. Many of the delegates came from organizations which wanted far more than the replacement of Abdul Hamid by another member of the same family, although most were willing to consider such a move as a step in the right direction. Actually, only a confirmed optimist could have expected the Congress to accomplish anything concrete, yet the interesting thing was that the main cleavage developed between different Turkish groups rather than between groups of different nationality.

The Congress was opened by Sabaheddin, who had been unanimously elected president of the gathering,[34] with an address in which he deprecated the fact that the existing régime in Turkey had departed so greatly from former Turkish practice in dealing with the peoples of other races and religions

---

[33] *ibid.*, p. 364; Story, *op. cit.*, p. 307; Denais, *op. cit.*, p. 40, states that he was responsible for obtaining the use of Lefèvre-Pontalis' home. Denais, secretary of "l'Association des journalistes parisiens," became a devoted follower and defender of Sabaheddin, and his partisanship must be taken into consideration in dealing with this subject. Fesch was also devoted to Sabaheddin, but his work, at least, is a mine of documentary information.

[34] *Pro-Armenia*, 11 (February 25, 1902), p. 53. A Greek, Sathas, and an Armenian, Sissian, were elected vice-presidents.

within the Empire. He was careful to make a distinction between the government and Turks in general, for, he said,

It must be thoroughly understood that the Turks who constitute today the majority in the Empire, ask nothing for themselves which they do not ask also, and in the same measure, for all their compatriots, Moslem and non-Moslem.

It is not proven, moreover, that the Ottoman Empire, from the début to its constitution, has never failed to respect the language, the customs, the religion of all the various peoples over whose destinies it presided? . . .

We reiterate: the reforms whose application we demand in our country and for whose execution we are working with all our power, we do not demand them for such and such a people, such and such a religion, to the exclusion of such and such others; we demand them for all the Ottomans without exception. . . .[35]

Having applauded the lofty sentiments expressed by Prince Sabaheddin, the delegates settled down to work and soon emerged with the following resolutions:

1. We reject all solidarity between the Ottoman peoples and the régime under which we have lived for twenty-five years, a régime of oppression, the sole source of the misdeeds which are committed in the Empire and which inspire the indignation of the whole of humanity;

2. We intend to establish between the different peoples and races of the Empire an entente which will assure to all, without distinction, the full enjoyment of their rights recognized by the imperial Hatts and consecrated by the international treaties, will procure for them the means of satisfying in a complete fashion their legitimate aspirations to take part in local administration, will put them on an equal footing from the point of view of the rights as well as the duties incumbent upon all citizens, will inspire in them the sentiment of fidelity and of loyalty towards the throne and the dynasty of Osman, which alone can maintain their union;

3. We shall apply ourselves in all circumstances to coordinate the desires of all the Ottoman peoples and the efforts of all the patriots towards this triple goal: A) maintenance of the integrity and of the indissolubility of the Ottoman Empire; B) reestablishment of order

[35] Fesch, *op. cit.*, pp. 367-368, quoting from the account published by the Congress of its deliberations under the title *Congrès des libéraux ottomans* (Paris, 1902).

and peace in the interior, an essential condition of progress; c) respect for the fundamental laws of the Empire, notably of the Constitution promulgated in 1876, which is incontestably the most important part and which offers the surest and most precious guarantee of general reforms, the rights and the political liberties of the Ottoman peoples against the arbitrary;

4. We proclaim our firm resolution to respect the international treaties and particularly the treaty of Berlin, of which the dispositions, insofar as they concern the internal order of Turkey, will be extended to all the provinces of the Empire.[86]

The old-line Young Turks, the proud remnants of the Society of Union and Progress, had come to the Congress with some misgivings, for they were not too pleased at the prospect of being a minority in a large gathering of "Ottomans," particularly when there was still a very considerable difference of opinion on what being an "Ottoman" meant. However, with the adoption of the above resolutions they began to breathe more easily, for the resolutions embodied their own basic principles, particularly in the third paragraph, drawn up during the course of a preparatory session for which Halil Ganem had acted as chairman.[87] The fourth paragraph probably was inserted at the instigation of some other faction; it may have sounded slightly ominous to Ahmet Riza's group, but if so it was not worth wasting too much energy to combat, for it was couched in very general terms.

When the full Congress met to pass on the resolutions, however, the worst fears of the Riza-Ganem faction were realized, for, as a contemporary account of the Congress sympathetic to their views phrased it, "a kind of mine was sprung on the programmes just described."[38] This "mine" was in the form of a proposal by one of the delegates that an additional paragraph be added to the resolutions, a paragraph calling upon the Euro-

---

[86] Fesch, *op. cit.*, pp. 368-370, and Denais, *op. cit.*, p. 40, note, reproduce these resolutions in full; see also, *Pro-Armenia, loc. cit.*

[87] Karl Blind, "The Prorogued Turkish Parliament," *North American Review*, CLXXV (July 1902), p. 44. Blind was apparently just as determined a supporter of Ahmet Riza as were Fesch and Denais of Sabaheddin.

[88] Karl Blind, "The Prorogued Turkish Parliament," *loc. cit.*

pean powers to intervene on behalf of the oppressed peoples of the Ottoman Empire. Over the outraged protests of Ahmet Riza and his colleagues this proposal was accepted, and the following "Conclusion" was added to the other resolutions:

Such being the principles upon which the entente is established, we are constituting a permanent Committee which will strive to make these principles prevail and will devote itself to the necessary overtures, with the signatory powers of the treaty of Paris of the year 1856 and the treaty of Berlin of the year 1878, in order to obtain their moral concurrence and a benevolent action on their part, having for its object the putting into execution of the international agreements stipulating internal order in Turkey, as well as of all the international acts flowing from the aforesaid treaties and their adaptation to all the vilayets of the Empire, in the manner most profitable to each of them.[39]

Once again Ahmet Riza found himself branded as a stubborn and pig-headed individual who refused to accept the verdict of the majority, and once again he stuck to his guns. He was able to insert the following minority declaration in the proceedings of the Congress:

In adhering to the Congress, we were hoping for fusion amongst all the Ottoman elements and we were expecting to profit from this force created by your union. We express here our keen regret at having been disappointed in our legitimate hopes.

The majority in the Congress has believed that in order to execute reforms in Turkey it is requisite, of necessity, to have recourse to the intervention of the Powers, and the spirit of the resolution made condenses itself after a fashion into this formula of the *benevolent action* of the Powers. We, the minority, convinced that the Powers are guided by self-interest and that this self-interest is not always in accord with that of our country, we have rejected entirely an action which infringes the independence of the Ottoman Empire.

Nevertheless we are not, as is pretended, hostile to Europe; on the contrary, one of our principal desires consists in seeing European civilization spread out in our country, notably its scientific progress and its practical institutions. We are following the road traced by her, and, even in our refusal to accept foreign intervention, we are inspired by patriotic resolutions of which all the European peoples

[39] Fesch, *op. cit.*, p. 370.

jealous of their independence have shown themselves justifiably proud.[40]

Ahmet Riza was not the only dissenter, however. The Armenian delegates, who represented well-organized committees with definite objectives, came to the Congress with their own interests firmly in mind. They were prepared to make use of the Congress if possible, but they were not disposed to subjugate any of their aims to the will of the majority any more than was Ahmet Riza. This was made extremely clear when the delegates from the Armenian Committee declared,

1. That the Armenian Committees are ready to collaborate with the Ottoman liberals in all common action having as object the transforming of the present régime;

2. That outside of the common action the Armenian Committees will continue their private action, it being well understood that this action is directed against the present régime and not against the unity and organic existence of Turkey:

3. That their private action has, moreover, no other object than to obtain the immediate execution of article 61 of the treaty of Berlin, of the memorandum of May 11, 1895 and of its annex, as well as the reforms mentioned in the memoirs remitted by diplomatic channels to the French government in the name of the Armenian Committees.[41]

It is impossible to blame the Armenians for their realistic attitude. They knew what they wanted, and their declaration was straightforward enough to leave no doubt as to what they desired. However, it is a little difficult to understand the response which the Armenian stand evoked from Sabaheddin and the other delegates, especially after it was brought out that the Armenians were not going to subscribe to any of the general resolutions of the Congress, including the statement which was

[40] Fesch, op. cit., pp. 372-373.

[41] Fesch, op. cit., pp. 370-371; Pro-Armenia, II (February 25, 1902), p. 49. The memorandum of May 11, 1895 was a scheme of reforms for the six vilayets in which the Armenians were for the most part located. It was not far-reaching enough for the English but was blocked by the Russians. The Armenians wanted to use it as a basis for establishing an area in which they would "enjoy exceptional privileges, and which would form the nucleus of a future independent Armenian Kingdom, and to this Russia would not and could not agree." Langer, op. cit., I, 163.

the very cornerstone of the Congress—the intent to transform the despotic rule of Abdul Hamid into a constitutional government.[42] The only point on which the Armenians were enthusiastically in agreement with their "brother Ottomans" was the one over which Ahmet Riza broke with the Congress—the question of inviting foreign intervention. Obviously Sabaheddin, who was the chief exponent of this policy, felt that this factor outweighed all other considerations, for, while the Armenians, who were in agreement with the Congress on this issue alone, were petted and coddled, the *Mechveret* group of Turks, who were in agreement with everything except this issue, were roundly abused for their attitude.[43]

In this connection the final pronouncement of the Congress makes interesting reading:

The representatives of the peoples of the Ottoman Empire who have taken part in the Congress opened February 2 [*sic*] at Paris, after having taken cognizance of the above declarations, protesting against the present régime of Turkey:
Undertake to work in common with a view:
1. To transform the present régime of government into a régime of liberty and of justice such that it will assure the reestablishment of the Constitution;
2. To recall to the European powers that it is their duty and to the general interest of humanity to cause the clauses of the treaties and international acts occurring between them and the Sublime Porte to be executed, in a manner to cause all the parts of the Ottoman Empire to profit.
On the other hand, the Armenians having declared that they are not able to take it upon themselves to associate their efforts with those of the other Ottomans for the realization of the desires expressed by the latter concerning the transformation of the present régime into a constitutional régime, which the Armenians consider inopportune

[42] See the final declaration of the Congress, below.
[43] See Fesch, p. 372, and Denais, p. 40n., and his "Annexe B." There can be little doubt that they are following Sabaheddin's views implicitly, for, as has been noted, both of these men were warm friends of Sabaheddin. There has even been some suggestion that Fesch was really only a "ghost-writer" for Sabaheddin, but the truth of the matter is that Fesch based his chapter "La Jeune Turquie" on information supplied by Fazlı Tung (Ahmet Fazlı Bey). For a discussion of this point, see the bibliographical notes.

71

and even contrary to their interests, the Ottoman members of the Congress, together with the Greeks and Albanians who have participated with them, have declared from their side in a great majority, that the divergence of views which has been produced on this particular point, will not prevent them at all from seeking the most efficacious remedies for the evils from which the Armenians suffer and to endeavor to obtain:

1st, The accomplishment of the legitimate desires of the Armenians, relative to the organization of the local administration of the provinces which they inhabit and of all the other provinces; 2nd, the establishment of a central government resting upon liberal ideas and which will be the best guarantee of national rights, as of the regular functioning of the provincial administrations and in which the Armenians will benefit by the same standard and in the same measure as all the peoples of the Empire.[44]

It is apparent from the mass of declarations, conclusions, resolutions, statements, and counter-declarations issued by the Congress of Ottoman Liberals that, as might have been expected, a number of forces were working at cross purposes. The national minorities of the Empire had nothing to lose by inviting foreign intervention in the affairs of Turkey and were consequently more than willing to subscribe to any demand for such action. The Christian minorities, exemplified by the Armenians, felt no attachment to a dynasty which was Turkish and Moslem, and the prospect that it might be made somewhat more palatable in the nebulous future through a constitution was hardly enough to make them accept it. The Moslem minorities, such as those Albanians who professed Islam, were beginning to. feel the sweep of nationalism as well, but they were somewhat weakened in their aspirations by the fact that they enjoyed better treatment than did the Christian minorities and because they had a religious bond with the dynasty that the latter did not possess. Such men as Ismail Kemal Bey exemplified this dual loyalty, and Abdul Hamid made great use of the Albanians in government positions.

In the midst of all this confusion stood Sabaheddin, who was

44 Fesch, *op. cit.*, pp. 371-372.

beginning to formulate his idea of an Ottoman Confederation in which the various nationalities of the Empire would have a great measure of autonomy and in which the main bond would be the dynasty. At the other extreme were Ahmet Riza and his associates who, as has been indicated, represented a Turkish nationalism which admitted only that the reigning Sultan was evil and maintained that the solution to everything was to replace him with another member of the same family and revive the constitution which had been suspended in 1878. The new Sultan would, of course, be Caliph as well, with all that this position implied, and there was little chance that the Christian minorities could ever hope to achieve anything like equality under this system.

These views were not new. Murat Bey had expressed them in 1897 shortly before he turned his back on the Young Turk cause, and Ahmet Riza had always been in substantial agreement with Murat on these fundamental concepts,[45] as well as on another major precept—the idea that the European powers were directly responsible for much of the dissension and trouble in Turkey.

With all these forces at work it is small wonder that disagreement arose in the Congress. One gets the impression that Sabaheddin, for all his noble sentiments and lofty ideals, was an ingenuous young man with a far from perfect grasp of the complexity of the problem with which he was confronted. Perhaps he had some idea of bringing the Armenians back into the fold eventually by conciliating them at this time, but it is more likely that he played into the hands of the Armenian Committees. Insofar as the *Mechveret* faction was concerned, it would appear that he antagonized them unnecessarily, especially since he accepted the potentially far more disturbing divergence in views of the Armenians.

Actually, the main stumbling block in the path of unity, the question of intervention, should have been anticipated by all the participants. There was no reason why the *Mechveret* group

45 See Chapter II.

should have regarded the introduction of this subject to the Congress as an unexpected "mine," for the sentiments of the majority of the delegates were well known.[46] In September 1901, for example, Ismail Kemal Bey had received the whole-hearted support of the Armenians when, in a letter to the *Matin*, he had praised France for severing diplomatic relations with Turkey and had maintained that all Ottomans, without exception, were ready to accept any action the French might take to insure honest and humane government in Turkey.[47] Ahmet Riza had reacted violently at that time, and there was no reason why it should have surprised him to encounter the same attitude at the Congress.

On the other hand, Ahmet Riza's views should have been equally well known to those who cried that he was changing his spots when he issued his denouncement of intervention. Paul Fesch, in his monumental work, *Constantinople aux derniers jours d'Abdul-Hamid*, insisted that *Mechveret* "had always been interventionist,"[48] but while it does appear that Ahmet Riza was somewhat confused at times over what was meant by intervention, it is certainly wrong to classify him as an interventionist.[49]

[46] It may be that they did not expect Sabaheddin to support this policy, although this is unlikely. However, the information available on Sabaheddin's ideas before this time is meager. Blind, *op. cit.*, p. 44, writes of the Congress with some indignation—and possibly surprise, "Finally the President, the son of the Sultan's brother-in-law, mixing repeatedly in the fray in favor of foreign intervention, succeeded in having that proposal passed by a majority in which not Turks but Greeks and Albanese were prominent."

[47] *Pro-Armenia*, I (October 10, 1901), p. 172. Ismail Kemal does not mention the incident in his memoirs. France broke with Turkey in August 1901, because Abdul Hamid attempted to gainsay the right, established by the capitulations, of French members of Roman Catholic orders to settle in his dominions without specific authorization and because certain French business interests were having difficulty in collecting debts. Later in the year the French obtained what they wanted through a naval demonstration and the seizure of the customs house at Mytilini. The whole procedure was, of course, most distasteful to Ahmet Riza and his friends, who found themselves far more in sympathy with the Sultan than with the French in such an affair, where the main issue was national pride.

[48] Fesch, *op. cit.*, p. 374.

[49] See, for example, the program (above, Chapter II), set forth by *Mechveret* at the beginning of its existence: "We are opposed to the substitution of direct intervention by the foreign powers for Ottoman authority." The writer

A more realistic approach to the problem by Sabaheddin might well have avoided much of the dissension.

In the last analysis the question is—and was at the time—almost purely an academic one and might well have been recognized as such by the delegates to the Congress. They could form committees, appoint delegations, and make representations to their hearts' content, but the classic Near Eastern Question would remain. The Armenians had been trying these methods for years and had eventually concluded that far more drastic steps were required. Sympathy could be attracted by any group which complained of the injustices perpetrated by Abdul Hamid, but it was another matter to secure the concerted diplomatic action which would be necessary to remedy the situation. Russia alone could—and would—block any attempt to resolve the problem on anything but her terms, and until she could obtain these terms she was quite satisfied with Abdul Hamid and not at all concerned with what he did to his subjects.

The only tangible result of the Congress, then, was a negative one—the accentuation of the difference of views of Sabaheddin and Ahmet Riza into a rift—and the Young Turks of Paris then settled into their respective grooves. A new organ carrying the name of the Society of Union and Progress was founded under the direction of Mehmet Ali Fazil Pasha, a member of the Egyptian Khedivial family, Ahmet Riza, Selânikli Nazim Efendi, Sezayi Bey, and Ahmet Saip Bey.[50] This new paper was called *Chourai-Ummet* (*Council of the People*).[51] Sabaheddin, who, according to one of his admirers, realized his

---

is admittedly handicapped by the fact that he has been unable to consult files of *Mechveret* directly, but the evidence is nevertheless strong that Riza was not in favor of intervention. See his articles in *Revue Occidentale*, sec. sér., XII (July 1896), pp. 93-98; vol. 23 (January 1901), pp. 53-57; etc. See also Tahsin Paşa, *Abdülhamit ve Yıldız Hatıraları*, p. 202. Nevertheless, Fesch's quotations from *Mechveret* show that Riza was somewhat prone to split hairs, for he would sometimes denounce intervention in one breath and demand with the next that the "concours moral" of the powers be turned on Abdul Hamid.

[50] Fesch, p. 376.
[51] This is the French transliteration of the Turkish *Şûrayı Ümmet*.

lack of preparedness to assume the rôle of leader of the anti-Hamidian movement, commenced to devote himself to the study of "social and political science."[52]

However, it appears that Sabaheddin, realizing that words were only words, soon began to feel that matters must be brought to a head in the fight against Abdul Hamid. Consequently, he, according to Ismail Kemal Bey, entered into an agreement with that gentleman, who was also discouraged by the lack of unity in the recent Congress, to precipitate a revolution in the Ottoman Empire.[53] This agreement must have been reached well before the end of 1902, for, as will be seen, the death of Damat Mahmut Pasha, in January 1903, occurred during the course of the preparations.

The plan which was evolved was simple enough. Marshal Rejep Pasha, an Albanian who was in command of Turkish forces in Tripolitania, was approached and agreed to carry out the operation, which envisaged transporting a portion of his army to Salonika, from which point he could call on his fellow Albanians for aid, or to some such strategic place as Bolayir on the gulf of Saros, the seizure of which would give him control of the Dardanelles. According to Ismail Kemal, it was felt that this would attract the attention of Europe and put such pressure on the easily-frightened Sultan that he would be forced to come to terms.

Having secured a promise of cooperation from Rejep Pasha, Ismail Kemal continues, he then laid the whole scheme before Sir Edmund Monson, the British Ambassador at Paris. Sir Edmund, after some reflection, provided him with letters to the British Foreign Office which he immediately took to London. Lord Lansdowne, the Minister of Foreign Affairs, was away at Sandringham with the King, who was entertaining the German Emperor, but, Ismail Kemal states, "in spite of his absence, I met with just the same business precision and quickness as were shown by Sir Edmund Monson."[54]

[52] Demetra Vaka, *op. cit.*, p. 122.   [53] Story, *op. cit.*, pp. 308ff.
[54] Story, *op. cit.*, p. 310.

Then, Ismail Kemal relates,

The following day Lord Sanderson, Permanent Under-Secretary for Foreign Affairs, invited me to go and see him at his private house, and I gave him a detailed explanation of our proposed course of action and of the nature of the protection which we asked for from the British Government, which was simply to protect us against any action which Russia might bring to bear to prevent the success of our patriotic action. Lord Sanderson promised to get into communication with his chief and let me know his decision. In less than two days I received a second invitation from the Under-Secretary to go to his house, and he then read me the letter Lord Lansdowne had written him on the subject. This gave a promise of support which was worthy of the traditional policy of Great Britain, though it was surrounded with a natural reserve dictated by the fact that our coup was not yet a *fait accompli*. I was greatly encouraged, and with the consent of Lord Sanderson I took a copy of the Minister's letter, which was in French, to show to my co-workers.[55]

From London, Ismail Kemal went to Cairo, where, as he had arranged with Lord Sanderson, he called on Lord Cromer to acquaint him with the situation. Cromer, he relates, "startled me at our meeting in Cairo with the remark that there was now no Turkish question," but was finally prevailed upon to agree not only that there was a Turkish question, but that it was to the interest of Great Britain to see it solved in such a way as to create a strong and friendly Turkey.[56]

Ismail Kemal's next move was to dispatch another compatriot of his, Jaffre Brejdani by name, to Tripoli to make the final arrangements with Rejep Pasha. He himself then set out for London once more and on arriving in Paris found Sabaheddin and Lutfullah greatly depressed by the death of their father, Damat Mahmut Pasha, which had taken place on January 18, 1903. Nevertheless, Sabaheddin accompanied him to London to make financial arrangements for the projected coup. Sabaheddin then informed Ismail Kemal that three Greek ships were ready and waiting only for his signature in Athens to start for Tripoli. So Ismail Kemal set off once more, he tells us, only

[55] *idem.*   [56] Story, *op. cit.*, pp. 310-311.

to find on his arrival in Athens that nothing was ready and that no proper understanding had been reached.

According to Ismail Kemal Bey, the great plan then collapsed because "We had to begin the work of getting transports all over again, and this work and the other negotiations took such a long time that the period when Redjeb Pasha could take his troops out of the capital for manoeuvers was past, the season being too advanced."[57]

The main lines of the story outlined by Ismail Kemal Bey appear to be essentially correct, but other versions of the whole episode portray Ismail Kemal himself in a far less favorable light. Detailed accounts are to be found in the strange work of Alexander Ular and Enrico Insabato, *Der Erlöschende Halbmond: Türkische Enthüllungen*,[58] and in Ahmed Bedevi Kuran, *İnkılâp Tarihimiz ve "Jön Türkler."*[59]

Ular and Insabato are unquestionably wrong in setting the attempted coup in 1908; they are also probably wrong in alleging that Ismail Kemal was in the pay of England, Austria, Italy, and Greece simultaneously; and it is little less than ridiculous to assert, as they do, that Sabaheddin "entered into the plan when the position of an autonomous Governor General of Macedonia was promised to him."[60] However, Kuran is in definite agreement that Ismail Kemal Bey played fast and loose with the money entrusted to him and that he approached all manner of people, including the Khedive of Egypt and the King of Greece, without consulting his associates.[61] In other words, the failure

[57] *idem.* The details of the plan appear to have called for Rejep Pasha to take his troops out on an exercise and then put them aboard ship at some distance from the capital.
[58] Frankfurt a. M., 1909, pp. 273ff.
[59] Istanbul, 1945, pp. 155ff.
[60] Ular and Insabato, p. 277.
[61] Kuran, pp. 159 and 164—where he notes "Ismail Kemal Bey wanted to carry through the revolution . . . by aristocratic channels." See also the "Annual Report for Turkey for the year 1908," *British Documents on the Origins of the World War*, v, p. 278, where Ismail Kemal, then a deputy from Albania in the first parliament after the revolution, is described as follows: "He has the Albanian intelligence and force of character, speaks French well, and ought, in the ordinary course, to render great services to his country under a Liberal

of the plot to get under way at all can probably be laid at Ismail Kemal's doorstep.

Ismail Kemal's most arresting statements, those concerning British interest in the plan and promises to support it, would appear to rest on a fairly firm foundation. Even without corroboration, his account of his dealings with various British personalities rings too true to have been made up out of whole cloth. Furthermore, Great Britain had, in 1903, absolutely nothing to lose by agreeing to put no obstacles in the way of a coup which, had it succeeded, would materially have increased her standing in Turkey, then at its very nadir. One detail which sounds particularly genuine is Ismail Kemal's delineation of the promise of support, i.e. "surrounded by a natural reserve dictated by the fact that our coup was not yet a *fait accompli*."

Quite apart from such speculation, however, is the fact that Ular and Insabato and Kuran are in substantial agreement that the British were aware of the plot and had even gone so far as to promise to conduct naval maneuvers to cover the crossing of Rejep Pasha.[62] Needless to say, British sources are silent on the subject, for it would hardly become one nation to admit that it had lent support to an unsuccessful attempt to overthrow the ruler of another.

Whatever the truth of the underlying reasons for its failure, the attempted coup was a fiasco which cost Sabaheddin much time and money. With better organization it might well have worked, but like the projected palace revolution of 1896, it slipped into the private limbo reserved for lost causes.

Mention has been made of the fact that Damat Mahmut Pasha died in January of 1903. This event brought a momentary

---

regime. He has practically no private means, and is reproached by his enemies with a certain tendency to looseness in money matters."

[62] Ular and Insabato, p. 279; Kuran, p. 156. It is admittedly impossible to place too much reliance on the former, and Kuran does not cite his sources. However, he was acquainted with all the principals in the drama and is a reliable authority. Nevertheless, note must be taken of the fact that while Kuran's two books on this period reproduce many valuable documents, he prints nothing of a documentary nature on this specific question.

truce between Sabaheddin and Ahmet Riza, and when the body of Damat Mahmut was brought from Brussels to Paris for burial in the Moslem section of the great cemetery of Père-Lachaise, Riza delivered the principal oration in honor of the memory of the man who had had the courage to stand up to the Sultan.

Abdul Hamid had never given up his attempts to get Damat Mahmut back to the shores of the Bosphorus. The steady stream of emissaries from the Sultan had never ceased to plague Damat Mahmut, who spent the brief two-year period of exile which culminated in his death moving from country to country as his presence became embarrassing to one government after another. Shortly before his death he was almost kidnapped by Munir Bey, who, taking advantage of the dying man's last illness, issued a statement that Damat Mahmut had told his doctors that he would like to return to his native land to die. Sabaheddin returned from Paris just in time to frustrate Munir Bey's plan, and Damat Mahmut himself rallied enough to declare that he had not abandoned his vow never to return to Turkey until the reforms for which he had fought had been achieved.[63]

Even after the death of Damat Mahmut Pasha the Sultan persisted in his efforts, for he made a desperate attempt to have the body brought back to Turkey. It was announced officially from the palace that Damat Mahmut had, before his death, made amends to the Sultan and had requested that his remains be conveyed to Turkey for interment in the family *türbe* or mausoleum. The two princes were deluged with forged letters, purportedly written by their mother, urging that this request be honored, and official demands were made of the French government for the exhumation of the body. Sabaheddin stood fast, however, and "the socialist deputies of the Chambre took up the fight, public opinion and the newspapers solidly backed

[63] "Le jour où le gouvernement de la Turquie comprendrait qu'il est nécessaire de poursuivre l'evolution du progrès réclamé par tous les Ottomans, sans distinction de races et de religions, je retournerais dans mon pays avec la plus grande joie. Sinon, non!" Fesch, *op. cit.*, p. 360, quoting *Mechveret* of January 1, 1903.

Prince Sabaheddine, and the government was forced to refuse the Sultan's request."[64] The Sultan, balked at every turn, made one last vicious attempt to discredit the memory of Damat Mahmut with his own people by causing it to be published that Mahmut had renounced the religion of his ancestors and was now buried in a Christian cemetery.[65]

For the next few years the history of the Young Turk movement is largely the story of the development of two main schools of thought, the one headed by Sabaheddin and the other by Ahmet Riza. The ideas of the latter have already been indicated in some detail, but Sabaheddin did not really crystallize his thought until after the unsuccessful attempt to unite all the Ottomans at the Congress of 1902. At this Congress he had made it evident that he was concerned with the welfare of all the peoples who inhabited the Turkish Empire, and we have seen that he turned from the Congress and the attempted coup of 1903 to a program of study which he hoped would equip him to understand better the problems which had to be confronted. For the next three years he remained in what Fesch describes as "an almost absolute retreat."[66]

There can be no question of Sabaheddin's sincerity. Like Ahmet Riza he took himself very seriously, and in addition he appears to have been motivated by the strongest possible sense of noblesse oblige. Thus he cast about him furiously, searching always for the key to the solution of the Turkish problem. He read the works of Frédéric Le Play[67] and was impressed by the

[64] Vaka, *op. cit.*, p. 123.

[65] *idem*; see also, Fesch, *op. cit.*, pp. 359-363 for the whole story of this episode. Actually, Sabaheddin was careful to observe all the proprieties, even to the extent of calling upon the imam of the Turkish Embassy at London to assist in the burial services.

[66] Fesch, *op. cit.*, p. 378.

[67] Sabaheddin's most devoted foreign admirer, Joseph Denais, gives the following enthusiastic description of the Prince's erudition: "Quand il s'exila, à 21 ans, il parlait déjà l'arabe, le persan, comme le français, qu'il parle comme un Parisien; on le considère comme un des premiers orateurs turcs, depuis les conférences qu'il vient de faire à Péra, à Bebek, à Smyrne, en Macédoine; l'histoire et la littérature française et étrangère lui sont familières; à vingt ans, il traduisit en turc, *Jocelyn* de Lamartine; il a tenu à étudier de bonne heure les divers sys-

doctrine of the family, religion, and property. The monumental *Nouvelle Géographie Universelle* of Elisée Reclus stimulated his imagination still further, and finally, when Edmond Demolins' *A quoi tient la Supériorité des Anglo-Saxons?* came into his hands, he felt that his prayers for guidance had been answered. This book, first published in 1897, had created a sensation in France and, to a lesser extent, in England, and had run through numerous editions in both countries.[68] In this work, Demolins, a disciple of Le Play, maintained in the main that education in the Anglo-Saxon countries had not, as in France, become a stereotyped preparation for the examinations leading to the inevitable civil service positions, but produced individuals capable of grappling with the problems of life. Home training, especially the relative lack of parental interference, was also instrumental in producing this individuality, he wrote, and the young Englishman or American got his start in life unencumbered by the fetish which made security and a thoroughly planned life the first consideration of the Frenchman.

The French, Demolins thought, were an example of the "Communistic formation, where man, untrained to individual initiative, is accustomed to rely on the community more than on himself," while the Anglo-Saxons, on the other hand, represented a "Particularistic formation, where the individual energetically maintains his independence towards the collectivity, where he is accustomed to rise through his own exertions, where, in short, individual action is uppermost."[69]

Pursuing this line of thought a step further, Demolins arrived at the conclusion that there are various kinds of what he called "State Patriotism." France, Germany, Russia, Italy, and Spain

---

tèmes philosophiques, politiques, économiques et il n'est pas plus étranger aux livres de Haeckel et Buchner qu'à ceux de Fouillée, Le Play et d'Edmond Demolins, pour lequel il avait un véritable attachment. Dans les sciences, il connaît assez les divers branches de la biologie pour faire un chimiste distingué, un excellent médicin. . . ." *op. cit.*, p. 76, note.

[68] The references made in the following pages are to the second English edition, entitled *Anglo-Saxon Superiority: to what it is due*, translated from the tenth French edition by Louis Bert. Lavigne (London, 1899).

[69] *ibid.*, p. 320.

represented, he felt, a state patriotism based on political ambition; this is most developed in "societies given to large public powers and to central administration."[70] Such an organization, Demolins reasoned, is conducive to war, for with a large bureaucracy surmounted and dominated by the rulers, the tendency is for the officials to have no will other than that of the state, which pays their salaries. War is often resorted to by the rulers in such a government—as a means of gaining or retaining power, as a means of distracting the people from internal difficulties, and so on.

Opposed to this type of "state patriotism" (or nationalism, to give it its more modern name) is the kind characteristic of the Anglo-Saxon countries, said Demolins. This is a "patriotism founded on the independence of private life," in which the individual will defend his fatherland to protect his own freedom.[71] For him the state exists only to facilitate his independence. "He does not consider, like the preceding type," wrote Demolins in words strongly reminiscent of present day discussions of totalitarianism and democracy, "that man is made for the Fatherland, but the Fatherland for man."[72]

In the Middle Ages, the author went on, Europe split up, and a "quantity of little *patries* took the place of the great Roman *patria*."[73] In France this form of society gradually disappeared and was replaced by a centralized monarchy, while in England it was preserved and can be observed today in that country and its colonies and in the United States. It is manifested, Demolins maintained, in the ease with which the Anglo-Saxon expatriates himself, a phenomenon attributable to the fact that the Anglo-Saxon takes his *patrie* with him wherever he goes and makes any country his own which affords him freedom. It is further manifested in the independent attitude of the colonies towards the mother country as in the British Empire, and by the complete repudiation of militarism.

[70] *ibid.*, p. 285.   [71] *ibid.*, pp. 291-292.   [72] *ibid.*, p. 292.
[73] *ibid.*, p. 293.

This is no place to attempt a criticism of Demolins' book. It had elements of truth and occasional flashes of penetration, but large parts were obviously based on superficial observation and even complete misunderstanding. In many ways it was a good analysis of the French bourgeois outlook, but the author evidently knew far more about his own people than he did about the "superior" Anglo-Saxons. By and large, his thesis, stripped of verbiage, was that the Anglo-Saxons were riding the crest of the wave for two reasons, the one dependent on the other: *decentralization* and *individualism*. Many would agree with him on these points even today, but it is another matter to acquiesce in the explanations Demolins made—or did not make—of how the Anglo-Saxons came by their individualism and how they developed the idea of decentralization.

Be that as it may, this work became Sabaheddin's bible. As the German Orientalist Carl Heinrich Becker remarks, Sabaheddin, like Ahmet Riza, now had his "body-philosopher" also.[74] Ignoring, as had Demolins for that matter, the influences of geography, environment, past history, and all the other tremendous forces which shape the destiny of any country, Sabaheddin seized upon the main tenets of Demolins' book and founded an organization to which he gave the resounding name of "Ligue de décentralisation administrative et d'initiative privée."

The purpose of Sabaheddin's league was to promote the correction of what he considered the basic defects of the Ottoman Empire. In Europe, Sabaheddin declared, it was generally believed that the Sultan alone was responsible for the miserable condition of the country, but, while it was true that the Sultan initiated the acts which were destroying his empire, the people were also in a sense responsible because they submitted apathetically. If the country were to be saved, the cause of this inertia, this social weakness, must be determined, and a "profound

[74] *Islamstudien: vom Werden und Wesen der islamischen Welt* (Leipzig, 1932), II, p. 355. For another criticism of Sabaheddin's ideas see Karl Klinghardt (ed.), *Denkwürdigkeiten des Marschalls Izzet Pascha: ein kritischer Beitrag zur Kriegsschuldfrage* (Leipzig, 1927), p. 115.

study" of the situation would undoubtedly reveal the fundamental causes.[75]

This "profound study," Sabaheddin was prepared to announce, had been made. "Our social weakness has its undoubted origin," he declared, "in our national education, in the lack of individual initiative which is its characteristic."[76] The lower classes, he continued, have neither the knowledge nor the capital to better their situation, and the great majority of the members of the middle classes turn toward careers as officials and as soldiers. Because of the scramble for power, honest officials with initiative are repudiated. In such a system, everything operates in favor of the retention of the corruption and anarchy which mark the administration and extend even into private life.

To eradicate this peril, Sabaheddin felt, it was incumbent upon the "intellectual youth" of Turkey who had acquired something of Occidental civilization to turn with all their ardor towards "independent and productive careers" in order to set an example for the people.[77] "But the omnipotence of governmental centralization being a perpetual obstacle to the emancipation of the individual," said Sabaheddin, "we must all, without a single distinction, unite our forces to replace the absolute autocracy with a constitutional monarchy, largely decentralized."[78] Such a decentralized régime, according to Sabaheddin, would satisfy the aspirations of all and assure the rights of Moslem and Christian alike to participate in local government; in addition it would render the Moslems a great service by pushing them out of the unproductive ranks of officialdom.

In line with these views Sabaheddin then laid down the following four-point plan of action:

1. To propagate amongst the Turkish people the taste for social studies, with the aim of stirring up private initiative and of leading the way to administrative decentralization.

[75] Fesch, *op. cit.*, p. 380; in general I am depending on Fesch for the exposition of Sabaheddin's views, for, as we have noted, Sabaheddin's connection with the author makes the book a firsthand source in this respect.
[76] *idem.*   [77] *idem.*   [78] Fesch, *op. cit.*, p. 380.

2. To seek means of arriving at an entente amongst the diverse races which constitute the Ottoman Empire;

3. To uphold the rights of the Ottomans in countries with a more modern civilization and to promote there a current of opinion in their favor;

4. To create in the interior of the country leagues and committees with a view to working for the realization of this program and to opposing themselves to the encroachments of an oppressive power.[79]

No party being complete without an organ through which its views can be manifested, Sabaheddin founded in 1906 the journal *Terekki (Progress)*[80] and entrusted its direction to his foster-brother, Ahmet Fazlı Bey (Fazlı Tung). A former student at the military academy in Constantinople who had been condemned to death by the permanent court-martial at Tashkishla, Fazlı Bey had, like many another, been sent to Tripoli instead and had managed to escape from that point and join the ever-growing colony of Turks in Paris. In addition to his duties in connection with the publication of *Terekki*, he also acted as secretary-general of Sabaheddin's "League of Administrative Decentralization and Private Initiative."[81]

Sabaheddin's general remarks and his specific program of action demonstrate convincingly how thoroughly he accepted Demolins' ideas and how fundamentally shallow his knowledge of the Turkish problem was. It is easy to understand how he might have been intrigued by Demolins' arguments, but it is difficult to entertain any great respect for his vaunted intellectual prowess when one notes how he simply took Demolins' main thesis and applied it bodily to an empire which was, as he himself pointed out, on an entirely different level of civilization. He might have added that it was an empire which had a completely different background and an entirely different set of problems to solve.[82] Nowhere in his program does he take notice

[79] *ibid.*, pp. 381-382.
[80] The modern Turkish spelling of this word is "Terakki."
[81] Fesch, *op. cit.*, p. 382, note (1). Fazlı Tung himself does not refer in his letter to this period of his activity, perhaps because of the fact that Sabaheddin was persona non grata to the nationalistic Young Turks who won out.
[82] René Moulin commences his *Force et Faiblesse de la Jeune Turquie*

86

of the tremendous complication presented by Islam, a factor with which Demolins was hardly concerned in writing of the Anglo-Saxons. Nowhere does he demonstrate that he had any understanding of the disruptive force of nationalism, although the Armenians had certainly brought the matter to his attention in 1902. His whole program was obviously based on the hastiest of conclusions, and one is tempted to conclude that his early life in Turkey had never given him an opportunity to study his own country and that his education had made him more of a European than a Turk.

Commendable, certainly, was Sabaheddin's determination to seek means of bringing the various peoples of Turkey together, and if he failed in this task it was not alone through his short-comings, for no one yet has been able to overcome the ancient hatreds and prejudices. Equally commendable, as has been pointed out before, were his determination to assure equal treatment for all the peoples of the Empire and his unrelenting opposition to Abdul Hamid. But the method by which he proposed to inculcate the spirit of individualism and initiative into the moribund Empire of the Ottomans was not commendable— it was naive. How could he have expected "to propagate amongst the Turkish people a taste for social studies" when most of them were illiterate peasants grubbing for their very existence? Such well-meaning nonsense tends to confirm the logical assumption that Sabaheddin had lived a very sheltered life in Constantinople and that if he did get out of the city it was only to the nearby family palaces at Chamlija and Kurucheshme.

As far as the fourth point of Sabaheddin's plan of action is concerned, it is difficult to say on the basis of the evidence available how far he had been able to progress in the organization of his leagues and committees in the interior of Turkey. Fesch, in alluding to the matter, preserves at first a very sug-

---

(Paris, 1910) with a quotation from Taine which Sabaheddin could have read to advantage: "La forme sociale et politique dans laquelle un peuple peut entrer et rester n'est pas livrée a son arbitraire, mais determinée par son caractère et son passé."

gestive silence but then relents enough to announce, "All that I can say is that the groups exist in the principal cities of the Ottoman Empire, even in the center of Asia Minor. . . ."[83] He adds that the groups were active enough to cause the Sultan some little annoyance. However, this is a question to which it will be necessary to return in a future chapter; suffice it to say now that it is not impossible that the wave of uprisings which took place in Anatolia in 1907 and 1908 had some connection with Sabaheddin's "League of administrative decentralization," for, as will be seen, the Society of Union and Progress confined its activities almost entirely to European Turkey at that period.

One other matter for which Sabaheddin has been reproached is his alleged sympathy for Roman Catholicism. The basis for these allegations is largely to be found in the fact that Fesch was a Catholic priest. One account even goes so far as to trace a connection, through Fesch, between Sabaheddin and the house of Orléans, a connection which, it is suggested, had all manner of sinister implications, including a tie-in with Ferdinand of Bulgaria, "the only reigning Orléans."[84] Actually, it does appear that Sabaheddin was made much of by French Catholics, but to censure him for associating with Frenchmen who were of the Roman Catholic persuasion is ridiculous, for it should have been evident, even to Sabaheddin's critics, that Frenchmen are more often Catholic than not. With respect to Fesch, there would seem to be little need to read sinister motivation into what at most was a natural tendency to keep on good terms with a man who had demonstrated his sympathy with the Christian minorities of the Ottoman Empire. The chances seemed to be good that Abdul Hamid would not live a great deal longer, and Sabaheddin would presumably be a man of some influence in Turkey thereafter. He could conceivably be of great use to French Catholics, no matter whether they were acting as Frenchmen

[83] Fesch, *op. cit.*, p. 382.
[84] Ular and Insabato, *op. cit.*, p. 288; Nazim Bey (Selânikli Nazim) is described as an "Orléanist agent" also, but Nazim was not a supporter of Sabaheddin. The remarks made about Ular and Insabato's book in connection with Ismail Kemal Bey's attempted coup of 1903 hold good here as well.

or Catholics, for France was the traditional protector of the Catholics of the Near East and the Levant. At the most, what Sabaheddin meant for the Catholics (and the French) was that if his proposals for decentralization were ever realized, their influence would be greatly strengthened in Syria and the Lebanon.[85]

Prince Lutfullah, Sabaheddin's younger brother, has not figured greatly in these pages, largely because Sabaheddin, as the head of the family, was the acknowledged leader and spokesman. Some time after the death of Damat Mahmut Pasha Lutfullah went back to Constantinople in disguise, presumably by agreement with Sabaheddin, to console his mother, Seniha Sultana. Much to his chagrin he was met on his arrival in Constantinople by officers from the palace who had been expecting him. Thus Lutfullah took up his residence on the shores of the Bosphorus once more. It is to be assumed that his mother was thereby made happy, and Abdul Hamid was apparently so delighted to have at least one of his recalcitrant nephews back under his thumb once more that he did not invoke the sentence of death that had once been imposed on the two princes and their father.[86] Lutfullah was subsequently sent to Paris by the Sultan in June 1906 in an effort to induce Sabaheddin to return as well, but it would seem that he made no great effort to insure the success of his mission. In any case Sabaheddin stood firm.[87]

During the years which Sabaheddin spent in study and reflection, the other prominent leader of the Young Turks in exile, Ahmet Riza Bey, had continued to wage war on the Sultan as he had been doing unremittingly since his flight from Turkey. *Mechveret* continued to seep into the Empire, and there can be little doubt that it was instrumental in keeping the spark of the Young Turk movement alive against the time when it could be fanned into flame once more. It was also important that Ahmet Riza and his associates were preserving the name

[85] On this question see especially, Martin Hartmann, *Unpolitische Briefe aus der Türkei*, p. 42 and note 33.

[86] Fesch, *op. cit.*, p. 377.

[87] *ibid.*, p. 407.

of the original Society of Union and Progress, which was to be reborn in the not-too-distant future.

Ahmet Riza, as has been shown, was under the influence of two main forces—the Positivistic philosophy of Auguste Comte, and Turkish nationalism. John Macdonald has described Ahmet Riza in the following words:

It will be long before Riza Bey's associates forget their 'tobacco parliaments' in the dingy little flat, in the somewhat dreary Place Monge, hard by the 'Latin Quarter' of Paris, in which during his long years of exile he planned the revolution, edited his little periodical the *Mechveret*, getting it smuggled, despite Abdul's spies, into every town, every regimental depot, in the Empire. To his Parisian friends, and to many of his compatriots resident in the French capital, he was 'Riza the dreamer,' 'Riza the recluse,' the student of philosophy, the disciple of Auguste Comte, never his best self except in the company of his literary and scientific cronies. His formula 'Oh, non-Moslem Ottomans—Oh, Moslem Ottomans,' contained, as in a nutshell, his political programme. The 'dreamer's' ideal was the fusion of all the races of the Empire, Moslem and Christian, into a 'new Nation,' with a centralized government on the French model; a 'New Ottoman Empire,' formed by amalgamation of all the races, secured from European interference by its military strength.[88]

As a good Positivist, Ahmet Riza was presumably not a good Moslem, for Auguste Comte, not content with reorganizing the world for his followers, also prescribed for them in matters of religion.[89] At the time which concerns this study, Comte's "Religion of Humanity" had enough followers in France, under the leadership of Pierre Lafitte until his death in 1905, and in England under the leadership of Frederic Harrison, to warrant the conducting of regular services. Nevertheless, Ahmet Riza spent a great deal of time and energy vigorously defending not only the Turks but their religion. He was able to convince him-

[88] *Turkey and the Eastern Question* (London and New York, [1913]), p. 54.
[89] Macdonald (*op. cit.*, p. 55) states definitely that Riza was not a Moslem. In reading about Riza's Positivist inclinations, one sometimes gets the impression that the term Positivism really implied that Comte was positive that he had the answers to all the problems of the world.

self that Mohammedanism had a greater similarity to Comte's philosophy than did any other religion and expressed the view in Positivist circles that for this reason Islam was better prepared to adapt itself to Comte's idea of an international religion —centered, like Comte's other creations, in Paris.[90]

The proof that Riza was a Turk first and a Positivist second, the attacks of some of his compatriots to the contrary notwithstanding, is to be found in the fact that he spent most of his time in Positivist circles defending his country. The pages of the *Revue Occidentale*, the French Positivist organ (and of the English *Positivist Review* to some extent as well), are full of his pleas for a better understanding of Turkey and the Turks. In 1905-1906, for example, Riza carried on an acrimonious debate through the columns of the *Revue Occidentale* with a fellow Positivist who maintained that the dismemberment of the Ottoman Empire was as necessary as it was inevitable and then rubbed salt into the wounds by insisting that the Ottoman Turks had absolutely no heritage of which to be proud in the way of literary, scientific, or other accomplishments.[91] Riza did not let his love for a brother Positivist prevent him from lashing back bitterly, and the argument was carried on for months without issue. Riza finally complained that after all he had done to render Positivism sympathetic to his compatriots, it was regrettable to encounter so unfavorable a stand against the Turks in the pages of the *Revue*.[92] The debate was ended, but not before Ahmet Riza had demonstrated that the international aspects of Positivism had not overcome his deep-rooted Turkish nationalism.

[90] See his speech on the occasion of the hundredth anniversary of the birth of Auguste Comte, *Revue Occidentale*, sec. sér., XVI (March 1898), p. 228. The theme of his address was the analogies between Islam and Positivism; among others, Riza made use of the following illustration: "Ne t'attache point, dit en effet le Koran, à une ideé par la simple supposition, sans en être sûr par la science."
[91] *Revue Occidentale*, sec. sér., XXXII (November 1905), pp. 444-445 and XXXIII (January, February, April, May 1906), pp. 109-112, 207-208, 331-336, 443-445.
[92] *ibid.*, XXXIII, pp. 443-445.

A glance at Ahmet Riza's program for the future of Turkey will show how deeply he differed with Sabaheddin. He used the word "Ottoman" freely in connection with individual inhabitants of the Empire, Moslem and Christian, as did Sabaheddin, but in Riza's vocabulary the word did not connote so much an individual with supra-national citizenship as a person who, if he was not already a Turk, must be hammered into a reasonable likeness of one. Like Sabaheddin, Riza envisioned the dynasty as the unifying force, and, again like Sabaheddin, he wanted the Sultans to be limited constitutionally, but, and here he differed sharply with Sabaheddin, he advocated a centralized government, run by good "Ottomans," by which he undoubtedly meant, in this case, good Turks.

Dr. Ibrahim Temo tells us in his memoirs that he once suggested to Ahmet Riza that a group of Young Turks meet weekly for the purpose of presenting papers on various aspects of the reforms for which they were all striving. The suggestion, he says, was adopted, and Temo delivered a paper on education in which he recommended that the state support religious instruction for the minorities. So coldly was this received by Ahmet Riza and his associates, Temo relates, that he never opened his mouth on the subject again. He notes that he was unable to convince Riza that he would never be able to instill a sense of national devotion into the minorities if he was not prepared to make certain concessions at the same time.[93]

Ahmet Riza was proud of being a Turk. The past glory of the Ottoman Empire was gone, he felt, but it was not too late to patch things up. Europe was responsible for much of the trouble, and bad rulers had made things worse. Correct these obvious faults, call the subject nationalities back to heel and make Turks out of them whether they liked it or not, and all would be well. The Turks, he declared over and over again, were the ones who

---

[93] Ibrahim Temo, *İttihad ve Terakki Cemiyetinin Teşekkülü* (Medjidia, Rumania, 1939), pp. 182-186. Temo states that in the same paper he pointed out that the Arabic alphabet was unsuitable for expressing the Turkish language and recommended the adoption of a modified Latin alphabet. The only result was that he acquired the nickname of "Latinist."

needed sympathy—all the other nationalities had their protectors. Once good government and fair treatment—by his lights—were restored, this nonsense about decentralization and even worse things would blow over. "Autonomy is treason; it meant separation," he said. "Our Christian compatriots shall be Ottomanized citizens. We shall no longer be conquerors and slaves, but a new nation of freemen."[94]

By 1906, the year in which the Young Turk movement commenced to reestablish itself within the Ottoman Empire, this, then, was the situation with the Young Turks of Paris. Sabaheddin and Ahmet Riza were the two most important leaders of the movement in exile, and Sabaheddin, as we have seen, did not represent, as did Ahmet Riza, the most powerful force which was germinating within the Empire, Turkish nationalism. Perhaps Sabaheddin was too far ahead of his day, although it seems more likely that he was not as acute as he might have been;[95] in any event his solution for the Turkish problem was not destined to have a trial. Ahmet Riza, for all his narrowness of view, his intolerance of other opinions, and his dogmatism, was much more closely attuned to the spirit of the times, although this was hardly a thing of which he was conscious. Nationalism was in the air, and nationalism, especially in its formative stages, is inclined to be narrow of view, intolerant of other opinions, and dogmatic. In the following chapter it will be seen how this spirit finally prevailed and culminated in the Young Turk Revolution of 1908.

[94] Macdonald, *op. cit.*, p. 55.

[95] It is quite likely that he also had an undue sense of pride in his own abilities. One of his contemporaries wrote bitterly of him in 1909: "He would not work as an ordinary member of the Ottoman Reform Committee, the headquarters of which were in Paris . . . he desired to be the sole leader of the reform movement. . . . But neither his age nor his knowledge of affairs could secure him a commanding position in the ranks of the Turkish reformers. . . ." Halil Halid, "The Origin of the Revolt in Turkey," *Nineteenth Century*, LXV (1909), p. 756.

CHAPTER IV

The Revival of the Young Turk Movement within the Empire—Joining of Forces with the Exiles—The Second Congress of Ottoman Liberals—Spread of the Movement—The Revolution

In July 1908 the world was startled to hear that the Turkish Third Army Corps, stationed in Macedonia, had revolted against the despotic régime of Abdul Hamid and that the Sultan had been forced to reinstate the Constitution of 1876. Somewhat later the news began to trickle out that the bloodless revolution had been directed by a secret society known as the Committee of Union and Progress.[1] It was therefore concluded by most observers that the years of patient work on the part of Ahmet Riza and his colleagues had finally been crowned with success, particularly as Riza then returned to Constantinople in triumph to become the first President of the new Turkish Chamber of Deputies.

In truth, however, the secret society which undermined the Third Army and precipitated the revolution was, at its inception, in no way an offshoot of any of the organizations of the exiled Young Turks of Europe; neither was it a direct heritage of any earlier Young Turk organization within the Ottoman Empire.

As has been seen, all organized Young Turk activity within the Empire had collapsed in the summer of 1897. This does not mean, of course, that each new class of students in the various military schools in Constantinople did not feel the impact of the new ideas and influences to which they were constantly being exposed, but the permanent court-martial still sat at nearby Tashkishla, and when an occasional group of students began to show signs of desiring to translate ideas into action, the Sultan's spies soon ferreted it out and with practised hand

---

[1] "Society" is a better translation of the Turkish word *Cemiyet*, but the term "Committee" now has the weight of usage behind it.

gathered in the conspirators to thrust them before the waiting court-martial. It is quite certain that no organization of any importance was ever able to survive in Constantinople in the period between 1897 and 1908, and it is very doubtful if very many attempts were made to form a society.

The first steps toward the organization of the military committees which were to effect the revolution were thus taken outside of the capital, probably by a young General Staff captain named Mustafa Kemal, later to become the founder of the present Turkish republic. Mustafa Kemal graduated from the General Staff Academy (*Erkâni Harbiye*) in January 1905. He had apparently been an active revolutionary as a student, for he was arrested on the same day that he was commissioned. He was eventually released with a strong admonition to forget his youthful indiscretions and posted to Damascus. There he soon found other dissatisfied comrades and in October 1906 formed with them a secret society known as *Vatan* (*Fatherland*).[2] Among his associates in this enterprise were another General Staff captain named Müfit Özdesh,[3] one Süleyman Bey, and a doctor known as Haji Mustafa Bey.[4] This last-named individual may well have been the actual founder of the society, but Mustafa Kemal, or Atatürk as he was to become known much later, was definitely a "charter member."[5]

[2] This is an important date, since it is almost certain that the Committee of Union and Progress in its final military form was founded after this group came into existence. While I had originally inclined to favor a somewhat earlier date, I have, on the assumption that it represents the most informed Turkish opinion, accepted the date given in the article "Atatürk" in the *İslam Ansiklopedisi* (Istanbul, 1949).

[3] At this time he was known simply as Müfit Bey; the surname was taken later when it became compulsory to do so. Müfit Özdesh became a deputy for Kirshehir in the new Turkish Republic.

[4] He later adopted the surname Jantekin and became deputy for Chorum in the Grand National Assembly.

[5] Some caution must be exercised in evaluating the importance of Atatürk in the formative stages of the Young Turk Revolution, for the Turks are over-prone to assign him the leading role, and his biographers are guilty of the same error. Actually the available evidence is very scanty. Atatürk's biographers—Mikusch, Armstrong, Froembgen, Ikbal Ali Shah, Wortham, Tongas, *et al.*—all derive their sketchy accounts of this period of his life from the

From Damascus the society commenced to expand, and branches appear to have been founded in such places as Jaffa and Jerusalem, the membership being drawn from the officers of the Fifth Army Corps, which garrisoned the Levant. It was soon decided that this area did not afford sufficient scope for their activities, however, and Salonika was eventually hit upon as a more profitable field of operation.

Salonika at this time was probably the most advanced city in the Ottoman domains, for its cosmopolitan population was less Turkish than European. Roughly one-half of the population was composed of Sephardic Jews who had long ago found in Moslem Turkey the religious toleration denied to them in Christian Spain. A number of them had been converted to Islam in the seventeenth century along with their leader, Sabbetai Sevi, the self-styled Messiah of Smyrna, and were now known as *Dönmes.*[6] In addition there were large groups representing every

meager collections of reminiscences and anecdotes published by the Turkish press in 1926—or from each other. The above-mentioned materials were translated and published in French by Jean Deny in the following articles: "Moustafa Kemal Pacha. I. Sa Biographie d'après le nouvel annuaire officiel de Turquie," *Revue du Monde Musulman,* LXIII (1926), pp. 146-167; "Souvenirs du Gâzi Moustafa Kemâl Pacha," *Revue des Études Islamiques,* I (1927), pp. 117-222 and 459-463. A decade later another series of articles on this phase of Atatürk's life appeared in *Belleten,* the journal of the Turkish Historical Society (Türk Tarih Kurumu). Of these, one by Âfet, "Vatan ve Hürriyet," *Belleten,* I (April 1937), pp. 289-298 (a French translation, "La Société 'Patrie et Liberté,' " immediately follows on pp. 299-309), gives very much the same account of the founding of the society in Damascus, but it may well have been based on the earlier material. Finally, the story is again repeated in the article (actually an 88 page book published as a separate fascicule) on Atatürk in the *İslam Ansiklopedisi* (1949). One still might be tempted to take it with a grain of salt but for the fact that confirmation is available in the disinterested account of General Imhoff, "Die Entstehung und der Zweck des Comités für Einheit und Fortschritt," *Die Welt des Islams,* I (1913), pp. 174-175. Imhoff, as was noted earlier, collected his information while it was still fresh and long before Atatürk became a national hero, and his story, derived from Turkish officers, tallies in the main with the above-mentioned ones.

[6] In 1666 Sabbetai Sevi was given the choice between death and conversion to Islam, not because of any sudden access of religious fanaticism on the part of the Turks, but because Ahmet Köprülü, the Grand Vezir, felt that he was creating too much discord among the Jews of Turkey. Sabbetai Sevi accepted Islam, and many of his followers, thinking there was some purpose in his move, did so as well. The name *Dönme* means "convert" or "renegade." There would

nationality of the Balkans, and in general the level of education was certainly far above the average of Asiatic Turkey.

The proximity of Macedonia to Europe and the complexity of its problems, which involved all of the Balkan nations and thus indirectly all of the great powers in one way or another, had long caused it to be kept under observation by the latter. A gendarmerie officered by Europeans had been imposed upon the Sultan in an attempt to preserve the precarious status quo. This made it considerably more difficult for Abdul Hamid to stifle the spread of ideas in Salonika and the other parts of Macedonia or to stamp out in his usual thoroughgoing fashion the organization which was actively working against him.[7] The relative ease of contact with the outside world was also important.

It is impossible to say how many of these factors were taken into consideration when the Damascus group decided to extend its propaganda into Macedonia. The most important factor was probably the hope for greater freedom of movement and less surveillance, for the fact that Salonika was more European than the rest of the Empire could hardly have been regarded as an unmixed blessing by men motivated by ardent nationalism. On the other hand, the very fact that foreign interference was most in evidence in European Turkey was undoubtedly one of the elements which recommended it as a center of activity, for the feeling was strong among the young Turkish officers that Macedonia must be rescued from these foreigners. Of course, once the movement was well launched the other factors came

---

appear to be some grounds for believing that the *Dönmes* clung to their old faith in secret, however. Abraham Galanté, *Nouveaux Documents sur Sabbetai Sevi* (Istanbul, 1935), pp. 75ff., tells the curious story that Abdul Hamid got wind of the fact that a number of *Dönmes* were active in the movement against him but feared to take steps against them because of his superstitious dread of their strange history. On the *Dönmes* in general see also H. C. Lukach (Sir Harry Luke), *The City of Dancing Dervishes and other Sketches and Studies from the Near East* (London, 1914), chap. IX, Leon Sciaky, *Farewell to Salonica: Portrait of an Era* (New York, 1946), chap. IX; and the article on the *Dönmes* in the *Islam Ansiklopedisi*.

[7] Cf. A. Sarrou, *La Jeune Turquie et la Révolution* (Paris, 1912), p. 14.

into play, and the nationalistic young officers did not scruple to make use of them.

Thus Mustafa Kemal, at that time Kolağasi, or Adjutant-Major, was either commissioned by the *Vatan* society or decided of his own accord to go to Salonika, his birthplace. He arrived there after slipping into Egypt and making his way from there by way of Greece.[8]

On arriving in Salonika, he was pleased to discover a number of sympathetic spirits, including some highly-placed officers, among the personnel of the Third Army Corps. He was encouraged particularly by Jemil Bey,[9] adjutant to the military governor, who managed to smooth over the awkward situation in which Mustafa Kemal found himself as a result of taking unauthorized leave from his post in Jaffa. A request for leave was put through the proper channels, and shortly after his arrival Mustafa Kemal was granted four months leave to restore his health.

These four months were all spent in the work of organizing a branch of the society which had originally been founded in Damascus. After feeling his way very carefully, Mustafa Kemal was finally in a position to hold a meeting of the first Salonika group. Present were the following officers: Ömer Naji; an artillery officer named Hüsrev Sami Kızıldoğan; Hakki Baha Bey, a former classmate of Mustafa Kemal who was at this time on the faculty of the Military School (Lycée) at Salonika; Major Bursali Mehmet Tahir Bey, director of the same school, a leading member of the Melami Dervish order, and a distinguished man of letters;[10] Ismail Mahir Bey, director of the Salonika

---

[8] Âfet, "Le Revolver Sacré," *Belleten*, 1 (July-October 1937), pp. 611-612 (a translation of the Turkish "Mukaddes Tabanca," which immediately precedes on pp. 605-610). See also, Deny, "Moustafa Kemal Pascha," *Revue du Monde Musulman*, LXIII (1926), p. 150.

[9] Jemil Uybadin, later Minister of the Interior and a deputy for Tekirdağ.

[10] Tahir Bey's most important work, *Osmanlı Müellifleri* (*Ottoman Writers*), appeared after this time in three volumes, the first of which was published during the World War and the last a decade later. He was known as Bursali (i.e. from Brusa) Mehmet Tahir to distinguish him from another writer called Bosnali (Bosnian) Mehmet Tahir. See Babinger, *Geschichtsschreiber der*

Normal School and subsequently deputy for Brusa; and Mustafa Nejip.[11] The organization appears to have expanded its name from *Vatan* to *Vatan ve Hürriyet* (*Fatherland and Liberty*) at this time, and its members swore an oath on the revolver of one of their number never to abandon their task.[12]

After the founding of the Salonika committee Mustafa Kemal returned to his post at Jaffa to mend his fences, for the Sultan's spies were breathing down his neck by this time. His friends in Jaffa had been covering up for him, and when a formal in-

---

Osmanen, pp. 406-409; Hartmann, *Unpolitische Briefe aus der Türkei*, pp. 94ff., 158, 173ff., 217f., 244.

[11] Âfet, *op. cit.*, p. 616; Hüsrev Sami Kızıldoğan, "Vatan ve Hürriyet = İttihat ve Terakki [Fatherland and Liberty = Union and Progress]," *Belleten*, 1 (July-October 1937), p. 621 (this article is in Turkish only); Imhoff, *op. cit.*, p. 174. There is some disagreement among these authorities as to the composition of the original members of this group: Âfet does not mention Mustafa Nejip; Kızıldoğan omits the names of Tahir and Ismail Mahir; and Imhoff was apparently advised that the original group consisted of Mustafa Kemal, Ismail Mahir, Hakki Baha, Tahir, "and a 5th officer, not named." See also, the anonymous article, "Die Türkei vor den beiden letzten Kriegen 1910/1911: Auszüge aus dem Tagebuch eines Diplomaten," *Deutsche Revue*, XXXVIII (April, May, June 1913), p. 49, which appears to have leaned heavily on Imhoff.

[12] Kızıldoğan, *op. cit.*, pp. 621-622, in a highly colored account of the meeting, describes how all those present felt the "hidden power" of Atatürk. According to him, Atatürk addressed the others as follows: "Friends, the purpose of assembling you here this evening is this. I do not see that it is necessary to tell you that it is a critical moment in the life of the country. All of you understand this. Towards this unfortunate country we have a solemn duty. To set it free is our sole aim. Today Macedonia together with a portion of Rumeli want to separate from the yoke of the fatherland. Foreign influence and power have . . . penetrated into the country. The Padishah is a detestable character, debased by sensuality and power, who will perpetrate any shamefulness. The nation is crumbling from injustice and tyranny. Death and complete destruction are the lot of a country which is not free. Liberty is the mother of all progress and salvation. History today imposes great burdens on her children. In Syria I founded a society. We commenced the struggle against absolutism. . . . I invite you to your duty, to answer an enslaving absolutism with revolution, and to overthrow an unfit administration which has become obsolete, to cause judgement to be passed on the nation—in short, to deliver the fatherland." To this Ömer Naji is said to have responded, "Mustafa Kemal, our protector, we shall follow you; even death, the hangman, martyrdom will not turn us from our decision. . . ." Such an account as this, in which later reverence for Atatürk is fitted into an earlier period, is hardly calculated to inspire confidence in the veracity of Kızıldoğan's testimony, although in general his main facts are substantiated by others.

vestigation was launched into his activities, his commanding officer blandly informed Constantinople that Mustafa Kemal had been on duty near Akaba in connection with the Turco-Egyptian boundary dispute in the Sinai region. Thus the authorities were forced to conclude that some other Mustafa Kemal must have been reported upon from Salonika.[18]

For some time after this episode Mustafa Kemal was extremely circumspect in his behavior, but he nevertheless started to try to obtain a transfer to Salonika. The transfer was obtained in 1907, but by this time the organization which was to bring about the Revolution of 1908 under the name of Union and Progress had come into being in the Third Army Corps, and Mustafa Kemal, although he became a member of this group, was only one of many. He was not, like Enver, thrown to the top by the happenings of 1908. He did serve as Chief of Staff to Mahmut Shevket Pasha in the march on Constantinople to put down the attempted counter-revolution of 1909, but he was never in the councils of the Society of Union and Progress.

The real birth of this latter organization, then, was a phenomenon apparently quite unconnected with that of the group founded by Mustafa Kemal in Salonika, although the two societies did soon merge, as will be seen. The organization did not immediately adopt the name *İttihat ve Terakki*, its first title being *Osmanlı Hürriyet Jemiyeti*, or *Ottoman Society of Liberty*.[14] Its first members were Rahmi Bey, later Vali, or Governor, of Smyrna; Talât Bey, a minor postal official who was to become one of the triumvirate which came to power in Turkey in 1913; Ismail Janbulat Bey; and Midhat Shükrü Bey.[15] Two others who became associated with the society in its infancy were the General Staff Colonel Jemal Bey—the *"Büyük"* (Great)

---

[18] Deny, *op. cit.*, p. 151. Such a situation could probably have happened only in Turkey where records were filed haphazardly and where family names were extremely rare.
[14] Letter of Rahmi Bey; letter of Dr. Akil Muhtar Özden.
[15] Letter of Rahmi Bey.

Jemal Pasha of the later triumvirate—and Fethi Bey, later Minister of Justice.[16]

This new society commenced to expand with great rapidity, and inevitably it encountered the group founded by Mustafa Kemal. Apparently Talât attempted to sound out a Major Naki Bey, who was already a member of the other group, and thus established a contact between the two.[17] Just when this event took place it is difficult to determine, but it would seem obvious that enough time had passed for the newer group to have outstripped the first in size and importance, for when the groups merged, the name of the *Vatan ve Hürriyet* society disappeared completely.[18]

As in the case of the first Young Turk societies, the new organization enlarged itself by means of cells or units of four or five members, each of whom in turn formed another unit of the same size. In this way no one man knew more than a handful of his fellow members and consequently was not in a position to betray the whole society. This was a typical Carbonari device, similar to that employed by the students at the Military Medical School nearly two decades before, but this time the inspiration may well have been derived from the notorious "Inner Organization" (IMRO) of the Bulgarians of Macedonia.[19]

Charles Roden Buxton, one of the founders of the Balkan

[16] Letter of Fehmi Janer. Janer's list of the four men alleged to have founded the society includes Talât, Rahmi, Jemal, and Fethi, but as there can be little doubt that Rahmi was one of the original four, it would seem only right to accept his statement as to the composition of the group. The others probably joined the first four very soon after the first meeting.

[17] Imhoff, *op. cit.*, p. 175.

[18] The whole matter of dating the beginnings of the Salonika movement is difficult. Kuran, *İnkılâp Tarihimiz ve İttihad ve Terakki*, pp. 207-208, reproduces portions of a letter from the Paris headquarters of the society to an unidentified man in Salonika, dated August 6, 1906, which reads in part, "Our greatest request of you is that, working in common with a few trusted friends of the same mind, you will organize a branch in Salonika." Kuran takes this to mean that no organization existed in Salonika before this date.

[19] This is one of those points concerning which it is impossible to be exact, but it does seem quite likely that such was the case. Charles Roden Buxton, *Turkey in Revolution* (London, 1909), p. 48, declares that the society "drew many hints" from the IMRO. This is substantiated by Fehmi Janer.

Committee, an English organization devoted to the problem of the Christian minority groups under Turkish domination in the Balkans,[20] visited Turkey directly after the Young Turk Revolution. Inasmuch as the Society of Union and Progress was carefully preserving most of its anonymity at this time he was unable to discover who its leading members were—aside from those who, like Enver and Niyazi, had unavoidably been thrust into the limelight—but he did gain an impression of the manner in which the society took in members. According to his information, a member of the organization

would offer to the intended proselyte to make known to him a secret of profound moment, but only on the condition that he would swear beforehand never to reveal it to another without permission. If he was willing to do this, and appeared worthy of trust, he was solemnly sworn, and the ideas of the Society were explained to him.

The next stage, however, was the most important, and it was invested with every circumstance of awe and solemnity. The form of initiation crystallised into a definite ritual. The man was blindfolded, and led to a secret place whose whereabouts was entirely concealed from him. The bandage was then removed from his eyes, and he found himself in a darkened room, perhaps in a lonely hollow of the hills, in the presence of three strangers wearing black masks. These administered to him the oath which was to become the rule of his life. Swearing on the sword and on the Sacred Book, he bound himself to devote his whole energies to the redemption of his country, to obey every order given to him through the channels of the Society, never to reveal its secrets, and to kill any person, however near and dear to him, whom it might condemn to suffer death. His eyes were again covered, and he was led back to the place from which he had started on the mysterious journey.

His fidelity was afterwards tested by a prolonged novitiate, during which his conduct was watched by the members, with none of whom, except his original introducer, he was allowed to become acquainted. Finally, he was affiliated to one of the local branches, which might consist of one or two hundred members. Of these, however, he was

[20] "The origins of the Balkan Committee are to be found in the widespread and uncomfortable feeling which existed at the turn of the century, that British policy was primarily responsible for the pitiful plight of the Balkan Christians." L. S. Stavrianos, "The Balkan Committee," *Queen's Quarterly*, XLVIII (1941), p. 258.

not permitted to know more than four. Five was the largest number which ever met together in a single group. For the purpose of communication, each group contained one "guide" who received the orders of the Committee from the representative of another group, and whose business was to pass them on without a moment's delay.[21]

The new organization, bearing in mind the quarrels and schisms which had arisen through the rivalry between Ahmet Riza and Murat in Paris and Geneva, determined that there should be no definite head of the society. It was decided instead to elect a new president for each meeting from those actually present.[22]

In Salonika, the center of activity, the conspirators were not long in discovering the usefulness of another organization—Freemasonry. Again because of the fact that it was difficult for Abdul Hamid to act in Salonika with the freedom he enjoyed in other parts of the empire, the old Freemasonic lodges of that city had continued to function uninterruptedly, although by no means openly, and their membership included many who welcomed the idea of overthrowing Abdul Hamid.

Consequently the Ottoman Society of Liberty found the Freemasonic lodges of Salonika admirably designed for its purposes. What seems to have happened is that the society made use of some, possibly all, of the lodges as meeting places, absorbed many of the members, and made good use of the techniques developed by the Freemasons in sounding out possible adherents. It is quite likely that the work of the society was speeded up to an appreciable extent by this encounter with Salonika Freemasonry.

[21] Buxton, *Turkey in Revolution*, pp. 44-46. This form of oath was also administered to new members of IMRO; see Christ Anastasoff, *The Tragic Peninsula* (St. Louis, Mo., 1938), p. 45, and J. Swires, *Bulgarian Conspiracy* (London, 1939), p. 76. Anastasoff also notes (p. 139) that Niyazi Bey, later to become prominent in the Young Turk Revolution, became more sympathetic towards IMRO after 1905.

[22] Letter of Rahmi Bey, who states that he was commissioned to draw up the rules of the society and that this rotating chairmanship was his idea. See also, E. F. Knight, *Turkey: The Awakening of Turkey; The Turkish Revolution of 1908* (Boston and Tokyo, 1910), pp. 108-109.

Of course, so simple an explanation as this of the role of Freemasonry in the Young Turk movement does not appeal to some writers, and it might be well to digress for a moment and examine the evidence with some care. Most of the literature dealing with European Freemasonry is, unfortunately, of so scurrilous a nature as to be utterly worthless. It is obvious, to be sure, that Freemasonry has been of some significance in European history, but for the most part the upheavals and even revolutions which have been laid at the door of Freemasonry have been carried out by men whose main motivation was nationalistic and liberal. The fact that they sometimes formed themselves into secret societies and made use of Freemasonic ritual does not mean that they sold their souls to occult powers dabbling in world-revolution, as some would have it. They had to meet in secret to meet at all, and they were often violently anti-clerical, for to them the church had become identified with reaction. The accusations of those who see only something sinister in Freemasonry are based on these factors.[23]

In Salonika—or for that matter anywhere else in the Ottoman Empire—it was necessary to go underground to discuss with impunity anything but the weather—and even that subject was not entirely open to discussion. Illustrative of the blighting censorship which prevailed in Turkey is the following account of a French writer whose articles were cut to ribbons so often that he finally sought out Rifat Bey, the director of censorship, and demanded to know of what he might speak. Rifat Bey replied,

"You may speak of everything."

"Of everything?"

"Absolutely. Of everything, except, you understand, of crowned heads, of foreign governments, of nihilism, of socialism, of revolution, of strikes, of anarchy, of liberty, of the rights of the people, of foreign policy, of domestic policy, of religion, of churches, of mosques, of

[23] For a reasoned judgment of European political Freemasonry, see D. W. Brogan's essay, "The Ruined Temple," in his *French Personalities and Problems* (New York, 1947).

Mohammed, of Jesus, of Moses, of the prophets, of atheism, of free thought, of the authorities, of feminism, of the harem, of fatherland, of nation, of nationalism, of internationalism, of republic, of deputies, of senators, of constitution, of plots, of bombs, of Midhat Pasha, of Kemal Bey, of Sultan Murad, of the crescent, of the cross, of Macedonia, of Armenia, of reforms, of grasshoppers, of the month of August, and of a few other subjects corresponding more or less to these."

"Good God, what remains?"

"What remains? Everything. The rain, good weather, provided you do not mention rain in August or the light of the moon. You may speak of the dogs in the streets, provided it is not to demand their extermination. You may speak of the authorities so long as you do not point out abuses. You may speak of his imperial Majesty to sing his praises. In short you have full and entire liberty to speak of whatever seems good to you."[24]

In view of the limitations placed upon them by the government, it is hardly surprising to find that many of the inhabitants of Salonika were attracted to Freemasonry—as they would have been to any such organization—for there were men of many faiths and nationalities in the city, men of some education and liberality, and Turkey was an autocracy second to none. To be sure, there were in Salonika many Jews, and many Jews were Freemasons. That, of course, was a highly suspicious circumstance to those who see in Freemasonry an attempt at world-domination by "international Jewry."

The result is, then, that in a very considerable body of literature, if it may be so called, we find that the Young Turk Revolution is just another aspect of this "world-revolutionary conspiracy" of the Freemasons and the Jews. Thus, for example, we find the authoress who had proved to her own satisfaction that the

[24] Comte Am. de Persignac, "Les Gaîtés de la Censure en Turquie," *La Revue*, LXVII (April 1907), p. 390. Despite the humorous vein in which his article is written, his list is surprisingly complete and accurate. Some of the prohibitions which seem to have no reason at first glance were based on touchy subjects. For example, Murat V was deposed in August 1876, which accounts for Abdul Hamid's suspicion of any mention of that month. See also G. F. Abbott, *The Tale of a Tour in Macedonia* (London, 1903), pp. 1-4, and almost any account of travel in Turkey in Abdul Hamid's day.

French Revolution was only the first outcropping of this conspiracy declaiming that

The Young Turk movement originated in the masonic lodges of Salonica under the direction of the Grand Orient of Italy, which later contributed to the success of Mustapha Kemal. Moreover, as we approach the Near East, cradle of the masonic system, we find the Semitic influence not only of the Jews but of the other Semitic races directing the lodges.[25]

Another analyst of the situation assures us that around 1900 the Grand Orient of France decided upon the removal of Sultan Abdul Hamid and proceeded to absorb the incipient Young Turk movement for that purpose.[26] Still another notes: "The Turkish Revolution, it can be stated emphatically, was almost entirely the work of a Masonic-Jewish conspiracy."[27]

One thing which played directly into the hands of the purveyors of such trash is the fact that in some cases the Freemasons have been just as eager to claim credit for things they did not do as the anti-Masonic writers are to give it to them. Thus, for example, the French Freemasonic publication *L'Acacia* seems to have preened itself on the importance of Freemasonry to the Young Turk movement, and this was immediately pounced upon by their opponents as positive proof of the diabolical nature of Freemasonry in general, and, specifically, in connection with the Young Turk Revolution.[28]

[25] Nesta H. Webster, *Secret Societies and Subversive Movements* (London, 1928), p. 284.

[26] Friederich Wichtl, *Weltfreimauerei: Weltrevolution: Weltrepublik: Eine Untersuchung über Ursprung und Endziele des Weltkrieges* (5th ed., Munich, 1920), p. 105. Elsewhere in his book, Wichtl refers to Wilson's Fourteen Points as "Das freimauerische Friedensprogramm Wilsons!" It might also be noted that there was no active Young Turk movement in 1900 aside from that of the lonely exiles.

[27] *The Cause of World Unrest, With an Introduction by the Editor of "The Morning Post"* (London, 1920), p. 143. This anonymous work consists of articles originally published in the *Morning Post* plus others by Nesta Webster. A great deal of it is taken from Wichtl, and the caliber of the writer is indicated by the delight with which he seizes upon the "Protocols of the Elders of Zion" myth.

[28] Cf. Wichtl, *loc. cit.*; *Causes of World Unrest*, p. 144; Lady Queenborough [Edith Star Miller], *Occult Theocrasy* (privately printed in France [1931?]),

This connection of Freemasonry with the Young Turks was given a semi-official airing soon after the Revolution when a correspondent of a Paris newspaper interviewed a Young Turk named Refik Bey. Refik Bey's statement would seem to make it quite apparent that the Masonic lodges were extremely useful to the movement, but this again has been seized upon as evidence of world revolution. He declared,

It is true we found moral support in Freemasonry, especially in Italian Freemasonry. The two Italian lodges, "Macedonia Risorta" and "Labor et Lux," rendered us real service and offered us a refuge. We met there as Masons, for many of us are Freemasons, but in reality we met to organize ourselves. Besides, we chose a great part of our comrades from these lodges, which serve our Committee as a sifting-machine by reason of the care with which they made their inquiries about individuals. At Constantinople the secret work that went on at Salonika was vaguely suspected, and police agents tried in vain to obtain an entrance. Besides, these lodges applied to the Grand Orient of Italy, which promised in case of need to procure the intervention of the Italian Embassy.[29]

---

vol. II, p. 585. Wichtl cites the article as having appeared in *L'Acacia* for October, 1908; the others appear to have taken it from him.

[29] *Causes of World Unrest*, p. 145, quoting from *Le Temps*, August 20, 1908, in proof of the author's belief that the Young Turk Revolution was a Freemasonic conspiracy. It may seem that the present writer is paying too much attention to literature of a fanatical variety in this discussion. However, the overstatement of the rôle of Freemasonry crops up again and again, as in the following melodramatic account in the popular biography of Atatürk by Harold Armstrong (*Grey Wolf: Mustafa Kemal; An Intimate Study of a Dictator* [London, 1932], p. 37): "Mustafa Kemal was initiated as a brother of the Vedata Lodge. He found himself in an atmosphere which he disliked. The lodge was part of an international Nihilist organization. It was full of men without nationalities who talked of the evils of Russia, where Jews were oppressed, and the joys of Vienna, where they were allowed to make money. They were furtive, unhealthy men, full of secrets and cryptic talk. Mustafa Kemal was conscious that he was caught into the threads of international finance and international subversive and subterranean organizations, but without knowing exactly what they were. He cared nothing for the international aims and troubles of Jews. He cared less for the Masonic ritual and spoke of it with contempt." (It is true, of course, that Atatürk later banned Freemasonry, along with all secret societies which might serve as centers of disaffection, but Dr. Ernst Jäckh has assured the writer in a personal letter that Atatürk thought it worth while to emphasize the connection in 1909.) Even so well-known an authority on the Near East as R. W. Seton-Watson was moved to state: "The

The above statement would seem to sum up quite well the role of Freemasonry in the Young Turk movement in Salonika; to assign to Freemasonry any larger share in the preparation of the Revolution of 1908 is not in keeping with the facts, for by no means all of the officers of the Third Army, who actually precipitated the Revolution, were Freemasons, and it is doubtful if all of the Young Turks in Salonika itself were affiliated with the organization. A large part of the strength of the Society of Union and Progress in 1908 was in the provincial areas outside of Salonika, where Freemasonry was not at all strong.

As far as the Young Turks of Europe were concerned, many apparently did become associated with Freemasonic lodges while in exile.[30] It is impossible to say how many of the exiles did so, but it can be stated definitely that at least two of the more prominent leaders were not Masons at any time: Ahmet Riza and Dr. (Selânikli) Nazim.[31]

In any event, it would definitely not have been in character for the intensely nationalistic Young Turks within and without the Ottoman Empire to have accepted the leadership of any international organization. While Freemasonry did enjoy a vogue in Turkey for some time after the Revolution of 1908, no serious student of Turkish affairs can accuse the Young Turk government of letting "international Freemasonry" or "world Jewry" dictate its policy from 1908 until the outbreak of the war.[32]

---

real brains of the movement were Jewish or Judaeo-Moslem. Their financial aid came from the wealthy Dunmehs and Jews of Salonica, and from the capitalists—international or semi-international—of Vienna, Budapest, Berlin, and perhaps also of Paris and London." (*The Rise of Nationality in the Balkans* [London, 1917], pp. 134-135; perhaps the date of publication had something to do with the author's statements.)

[30] Personal letter to the author from Dr. Ernst Jäckh, dated February 5, 1941.

[31] Personal letter to the author from Dr. Riza Tevfik, dated May 16, 1941.

[32] A very good illustration is afforded by the career of Emmanuel Carasso Efendi. Carasso, a Jew of Salonika, was Grand Master of the lodge known as "Macedonia Risorta" and is credited by some with having conceived the idea of inviting the Young Turks to meet in the Masonic lodges. (Cf. the obituary notice on Carasso in the London *Times*, June 8, 1934, p. 19; N. Nicolaidès,

Freemasonry was by no means the only secret or semi-secret organization which contributed to the growth of the Young Turk movement after its revival inside the Ottoman Empire, for some of the dervish orders of Turkey were apparently made use of in much the same manner as the Masonic lodges.

Of the Turkish dervish orders, by far the largest and most influential was that of the Bektashis, whose membership has been estimated to have embraced, in one way or another, at least ten per cent of the population of Turkey.[33] Other estimates suggest that as much as a third of Anatolian Turkey was under the influence of the Bektashi dervish order,[34] but in both cases it must be borne in mind that a very large percentage of the membership was composed of illiterate peasants and almost as illiterate *sheyhs*. Nevertheless, the order did attract many Turkish liberals and nationalists, for the Bektashis were the most Turkish in spirit of all the dervish orders. In contrast to the Mevlevi order (the famous "Whirling Dervishes"), for example, the Bektashis clung to the Turkish language and Turkish forms in their literature all during the period when the cultural life of the Turks was largely dominated by the "classical" influences of Persian and Arabic.[35]

Une Année de Constitution: 11/24 juillet 1908—11/24 juillet 1909 [Brussels, 1909], p. 155; Abraham Galanté, *Turcs et Juifs: Étude historique, politique* [Istanbul, 1932], p. 89. Nicolaidès was for some years editor of the pro-Abdul Hamid weekly *L'Orient* published in Brussels and was apparently convinced that Freemasonry was out to de-Moslemize the Turks). Carasso later became quite prominent in the Society of Union and Progress, was one of the delegation which apprised Abdul Hamid of his deposition in 1909, and was a member of the Turkish Parliament. In Parliament he, like the other Jewish members, was always careful to be a Turk first and foremost, which is the traditional attitude of the Turkish Jew. He evidently lined his pockets during this period (Cf. Henry Wickham Steed, *Through Thirty Years 1892-1922* [Garden City, N.Y., 1925], vol. I, pp. 375-376) in common with many pure Turks, but in matters affecting Jews in the Ottoman domains he invariably espoused the Turkish view. He supported, for example, even the harshest anti-Zionist measures. See in this respect S. M. Dubnow, *Die Neueste Geschichte des jüdischen Volkes* (Berlin, 1920-1923), vol. III, pp. 540-541.

[33] John Kingsley Birge, *The Bektashi Order of Dervishes* (London and Hartford, Conn., 1937), p. 16. This is the most complete study of the Bektashis available in any language.

[34] *ibid.*, p. 15.

[35] The discussion of the role of the Bektashis in the Young Turk movement

Because of its Turkish national character Bektashi literature figures prominently in present-day Turkish anthologies and histories of Turkish literature, although little attention had been paid to it by the relatively few European students of Turkish literature. Most Turkish literature was, until the middle of the nineteenth century, so under the domination of Persian style and so interspersed with Persian and Arabic words as to be unintelligible to all but the well-educated. Indeed, the more unintelligible a work was, the greater the erudition of its writer was considered to be. Even after the modern school of Turkish literature began to shed its Persian shackles, it did so under the influence of Western ideas and was merely aping another foreign style, in this case the French. Thus the voluminous Bektashi literature considerably antedated the national cultural renaissance which had its beginnings with Ziya Gökalp and came to full flowering after the establishment of the Turkish Republic in 1923.

In its doctrines and beliefs the Bektashi order is fundamentally liberal. It is neither orthodox Sunnite nor orthodox Shiite. It draws, rather, from a variety of sources, and the beliefs of individuals within the order ranged from "crudest superstition . . . to a definitely materialistic atheism."[36] It has been suggested by some writers that a connection existed between European Freemasonry and the Bektashi order. Richard Davey,[37] writing in 1897, remarks that he had heard it said that the order was "affiliated to some of the French Masonic Lodges," and as early as 1867 Brown[38] noted that some of his Moslem friends had become Freemasons in Europe. Of the Bektashis he has the following to say:

is taken in large part from the author's article "The Bektashi Dervishes and the Young Turks," *Moslem World*, XXXII (January 1942), pp. 7-14, with certain additions and modifications based on information acquired since the publication of the article.

[36] Birge, *op. cit.*, p. 87.

[37] *The Sultan and his Subjects* (New York, 1897), vol. I, p. 97. A later edition (1907) adds nothing to his information on the Bektashis.

[38] John P. Brown, *The Darvishes* (London, 1927), p. 64.

It is rather strange that the Darvishes of the Baqtāshī order consider themselves quite the same as the Freemasons, and are disposed to fraternise with them. The name of Freemasonry in the Turkish language is *farmāson*, and is one of great reproach. It signifies atheism of the most condemnable character, and this may be said of the Baqtāshīs, who, from some reason or other not quite clear to me, are held in small repute among other Mussulmans, even those belonging to the other Darvish Orders.[39]

On the same subject, another writer on Turkey says of the Bektashis:

In association with the Janissaries they played, during the eighteenth and early nineteenth century, much the same part in the Ottoman reform movement as did Freemasonry in European reform movements. They were, in fact, affiliated with French Freemasonry. Fazil Bey, a friend of Voltaire, remodelled the Order, so that it remained the organization of the Young Turkey movement for over a century. Its activities were philosophical, literary, scientific, and political, all with a national *arrière-pensée*.[40]

Richard Davey also states that a member of the order, whom he calls variously Fazil Bey and Izet Bey, was influenced by Voltaire, and that "on his return to Constantinople he introduced into the order, already a secret society, certain philosophical, even free-thinking views, which, in due time had a prodigious influence on the entire body."[41]

It may be assumed, then, that the Bektashis of Turkey had some concept of national feeling and that they were liberal enough in their outlook to attract adherents of many persuasions. Even women were accorded equality within the order, which gave rise to many dark rumors, some of which may have been based on fact.

Another reason for supporting the Young Turk movement may have existed in the fact that in regard to the Caliphate the Bektashis tended towards the Shiite doctrine of the Imamate,

[39] *idem.*
[40] George Young, *Constantinople* (London and New York, [1925?]), p. 198.
[41] Davey, *op. cit.*, vol. I, p. 156; see also, p. 96.

which did not dispose them favorably towards the claims of the Ottoman Sultans. Birge[42] suggests that the Bektashis hampered Selim I in his campaign against Shah Ismail of Persia in 1514 because of their secret sympathy for the Shiite Persians. Thus it may be that Abdul Hamid's attempt to revive the importance of the Caliphate was to some extent responsible for stirring up the opposition of the Bektashis.

In 1931, six years after the abolition of all dervish orders in the Turkish Republic, Ziya Bey, a Bektashi himself, published a series of articles on Bektashism.[43] His conclusion was that the Republic had completed the reforms for which the order had always striven and had thereby removed the need for the order. These reforms included the abolition of the Caliphate, the emancipation of women, and the dampening of religious fanaticism.[44]

It would seem that the Bektashis were not always guided by altruism, however. Hasluck[45] was of the opinion that the Bektashis "aimed at an ultimate religious supremacy in the countries touched by their propaganda," and that they still hoped at the time of the Revolution of 1908 to establish a Bektashi state in Albania.[46] He suggests further that Abdul Hamid became suspicious of the Bektashis at the time of the Albanian national movement of 1880-1881, when the possibility of ceding part of southern Albania to Greece arose. Whether Turkish Bektashis were completely in sympathy with the aspirations of their Albanian coreligionists is a debatable question, but these evidences of Bektashi political activity are none the less of interest.

Of still more interest is the fact that Hasluck seems to have heard that there existed some bond between the Bektashis and

[42] *op. cit.*, p. 67 and p. 159.

[43] "Bektaşilik," printed in forty installments from January 26 to March 8, 1931, in the Istanbul newspaper *Yeni Gün*. Cited by Birge, p. 20.

[44] How sincere he was is difficult to say. He may only have been paying lip service to the government in declaring that the order's *raison d'être* no longer existed.

[45] F. W. Hasluck, *Christianity and Islam under the Sultans* (Oxford, 1929), vol. I, p. 438.

[46] *ibid.*, p. 438, note 4: "This I have on good Bektashi authority."

the Young Turks, for scattered through his work are references to that effect.[47] It is certainly definite that a number of Young Turks were members of the Bektashi order and that some were both Freemasons and Bektashis—Talât Pasha, Riza Tevfik, and the *Sheyhülislam* Musa Kâzim Efendi were all in this category.[48] But it is also doubtful if support of the Young Turk program was ever part of Bektashi dogma; that is to say, as in the case of Freemasonry, Bektashism simply attracted men who were equally attracted to the program of the Young Turks—or to the simple proposition of overthrowing Abdul Hamid and establishing a more liberal régime in the Ottoman Empire.

It is equally clear that the Society of Union and Progress did not have any definite understanding with any of the dervish orders but was glad to make use of them in any way possible. It does appear, however, that both the Bektashis and Mevlevis gave aid and comfort to members of the society exiled to Anatolia.[49]

One other dervish order is worthy of mention in this con-

---

[47] Hasluck, *op. cit.*, vol. I, p. 595; p. 620.

[48] Letter from Riza Tevfik cited above. This interesting letter is worth quoting in part: "The Bektashis are indeed, the most liberal dervishes among all other secret (esoteric) sects. All of them are nonconformists towards the State Religion which is (sunnite-ortodox!). From the beginning of the Turkish Empire this sect, as many other ones, was recognized and respected. All the Janissaries were bektashis; after the degeneration of this famous military organization, Sultan Mahmood II annihilated them all, including the civil members and the Sheikhs of this sect, because of their insolent and stubborn resistence against any kind of reform. Yet there are a lot of them in Turkey; the great majority of the Bektashi fathers (viz: Sheikhs!) and the dervishes are absolutely illiterate, but in Stamboul and other centers of culture there are a good many bektashis, high ranked and cultured people. I know personally some vizirs, one feldmarshal, an Ambassador, many judges, writers, poets, etc. and two Sheikh ul islams at least, the one (Mousa Kazim effendi) was a member of the Cabinet ûnder Talat pasha (the leader of the Com. U. and progress); was like me and Talat pasha a Bektashi and a master mason at the same time. So it is true that all the bektashi confraternity, had already quite a good disposition of mind to welcome any political revolution and social reform favouring a full liberty of creed and a much more tolerable administration for Turkey. The revolutionary Committee had in Stamboul some bektashis among its members; nearly all the bektashis helped the committee to succeed in its aims." Riza Tevfik's spelling and punctuation have been left unchanged.

[49] Letter of Fehmi Janer.

nection, the Melami order. It has already been noted that Bursalı Mehmet Tahir Bey, one of the first members of the *Vatan ve Hürriyet* society in Salonika, was a prominent member of that order.[50] After he joined, "precisely through the character of Tahir Bey as a Melami the conspirator group sustained a significant increase, for he commanded so much respect among the brothers that all joined without hesitation as soon as they heard that he stood at the head."[51] This, of course, was a matter of personalities, but the Melami order was, like the Bektashi, liberal enough to attract men of Tahir Bey's stamp. Like the Bektashis also, the Melamis were popularly supposed to have had Freemasonic beliefs.[52]

In the other cities and towns of Macedonia and in the countryside, wherever garrisons of Turkish troops were to be found, the revolutionary society commenced to spread until centers of disaffection were to be found in all parts of European Turkey. Monastir (Bitolj) soon became a center second only to Salonika in importance under the direction of Bursalı Tahir, Major Süleyman Askerî, Major Vehip (later Pasha), and Lieutenant Atif.[53] Branches quickly sprang up in the neighboring towns: at Resna (Resan) on Lake Presba under Adjutant Major Niyazi Bey, who was later to become one of the most widely publicized heroes of the Revolution of 1908; at Ohrid under Adjutant Major Eyüp Sabri, who was also to become well known; at Üsküb (Skoplje) under Lieutenant Colonel Galip Bey (later Pasha); and at Gevgeli under Ömer Fevzi Mardin. Farther to the east nuclei were established at Seres (Serrai) under Captain Ali Bey, and at Adrianople under Ismet Inönü, later president of the Turkish Republic, together with the late Kâzim

---

[50] See above, Chapter IV.

[51] Martin Hartmann, *Unpolitische Briefe aus der Türkei*, p. 178.

[52] Brown, *op. cit.*, p. 64 and pp. 225ff.

[53] Letter of Fehmi Janer. The last named individual, Atif, is presumably identical to the Atif who assassinated Shemsi Pasha in July 1908, an event which was one of the opening rounds of the Revolution. Cf. letter of Ömer Fevzi Mardin. The Istanbul newspaper, *La Republique*, in an obituary notice on February 22, 1949, credits Ali Çetinkaya, one-time Minister of Public Works under Atatürk, with the leadership of the Monastir group.

Karabekir Pasha, Seyfi Pasha, and Hüseyn Kadri Bey. Drama and other towns also had centers.[54]

Each town or village acted as a headquarters for the surrounding countryside, and as a center for the constant work of proselytizing and the dissemination of propaganda. The more remote the village, the more open was the work of the committees. Adherents were obtained in steadily increasing numbers. The great majority was from the officer corps of the 3rd Army at first, but others were taken in as well. Within a relatively short time it was difficult to find a Turkish officer in all European Turkey who was not pledged to overthrow the government he served.

The causes of this disaffection in the Turkish officer corps are not to be found in nationalism alone. Under Abdul Hamid the army had great cause for dissatisfaction in matters more immediate and personal than the rather remote concept of national pride, although this factor was undoubtedly of great importance to most. Nevertheless, other considerations were undoubtedly responsible for causing many a young officer to turn to any group which held out a promise of improvement.

In the history of the Ottoman Empire the army has always played an extremely important role, both as an instrument of aggression and as a police force to maintain the control of the Turkish overlords over their subject peoples. Half a century ago Sir Charles Eliot wrote

> The Turkish army is not so much a profession, or an institution necessitated by the fears and aims of the Government, as the active but still quiet [sic] normal state of the Turkish nation.[55]

Another writer declared in 1908, "The whole Ottoman race is an army permanently encamped upon its conquests."[56]

Other observers also have commented on the fact that the Turks had no real roots in their own country. Eliot suggests

[54] Letters of Ömer Fevzi Mardin, Rahmi Bey, and Fehmi Janer.
[55] *Turkey in Europe* (new edn., London, 1908), p. 93.
[56] "Viator," "The Turkish Revolution," *Fortnightly Review*, XC (September 1908), p. 365.

that the explanation is to be found in the nomadic origins of the Ottoman Turks.[57] But whatever the explanation, it is true that army life was a normal one for the Turk, and it is also true that the army was vitally necessary to hold the Empire together —particularly as it was governed by Abdul Hamid.

Abdul Hamid must have realized this, yet under his rule the army, which did not mind hardships and a standard of living far below that of most armies, had increasingly great cause for dissatisfaction. From the first the Sultan had been afraid of his army, as was demonstrated almost immediately by his unwillingness to give sufficient power to any of his generals during the war with Russia. For the rest of his reign the neurotic ruler appears to have been torn between the desire to maintain a strong army and the fear of allowing it to become too powerful.

In even worse plight was the navy, which was allowed to rot where it was penned up behind two bridges in the Golden Horn. Abdul Hamid's palace looked down on the Bosphorus, and he could not abide the thought of being within the range of ships' guns. So he caused vital parts of the machinery to be removed as soon as a new naval vessel was acquired (as a number were during his reign) and then stranded them in the Golden Horn. Under no circumstances was ammunition allowed aboard a Turkish naval vessel. Typical of Turkish warships at this period was the ill-fated *Ertuğrul* which was lost off the coast of Japan in 1889. The Sultan had dispatched the vessel, against the advice of Turkish and European experts, to carry a decoration to the Mikado, and the ship apparently simply fell apart during a storm.[58]

In the army promotion was rarely accorded on the basis of ability. The intolerable espionage system was extended to the army, and the surest way to earn preferment was to submit reports on fellow officers. Pay was constantly in arrears, and the

[57] *op. cit.*, p. 91.
[58] Wladimir Giesl, *Zwei Jahrzehnte im Nahen Orient* (Berlin, 1927), p. 49f., gives the whole tragi-comic story of this episode. Giesl was the Austro-Hungarian military attaché in Constantinople and at various Balkan capitals for many years.

common practice among officers was to discount the pay due them to speculators who could make a profit by greasing a few palms in the capital in order to secure payment of the debts. Thus, unless he had private means, the Turkish officer was likely to be nearly as down-at-the-heels as the common soldier.

Of some importance also was the fact that Turkish officers were beginning to have more contact with foreign officers. It has already been noted that German military missions had had some influence on the Turkish army, even though Abdul Hamid, with typical indecision, did his best to emasculate the missions after agreeing to accept them.[59] After the Mürzsteg agreements of 1903, which provided for the establishment of a European gendarmerie in Macedonia, the officers of the 3rd Army were constantly being thrown in contact with French, English, Italian, Austrian, and Russian officers. Despite the fact that intercourse with the foreign officers laid them open to suspicion, many of the Turkish officers were willing to take the risk of mingling with their European confreres, and the effects of this association were soon apparent. Opportunities for education were greatly increased, and the young Turkish officers were made aware of many things which had been closed to them before. The better ones were avid and eager students. Enver Bey, for example, was particularly attached to the Austro-Hungarian officers who were stationed in the Vilayet of Kossovo (Üsküb) and took advantage of their friendship to study military tactics and German.[60]

The association produced other effects on the young Turkish officers as well. They could not help but feel shame when they contrasted their shabby uniforms and their menial status under

[59] Giesl notes (pp. 48-49) that the German instructors were not allowed in the Turkish barracks and could not even fire the guns whose use they were supposed to teach. Even the head of the military mission, Baron von der Goltz, was not exempt. Giesl tells the story that von der Goltz made a new map of Constantinople and vicinity only to have the police break in and seize it.

[60] Gustav Hubka, "Die Reformaktion in Makedonien in den Jahren 1320-1324 (1904-1908)," *Streffleurs Militärische Zeitschrift* (June 1909), p. 924. See also Hubka's book, *Die Österreichisch-Ungarische Offiziersmission in Makedonia 1903-1909* (Vienna, 1910), pp. 95ff.

Abdul Hamid with the resplendent dress and the relatively pleasant life of the European officers.[61] To be sure, their feelings were mixed, for while they envied and admired the gendarmerie officers, they also resented their very presence in a Turkish province. Thus there was a growing determination to get rid of them along with an almost pathetic desire to emulate them.

It is interesting to note that, despite their close association with Turkish officers who were almost without exception members of the Ottoman Society of Liberty or Society of Union and Progress, the foreign officers in the international gendarmerie in Macedonia had no knowledge of the vast revolutionary network which was growing under their very noses. One or two individuals did receive vague hints of activity on the very eve of the Revolution, but apparently no importance was attached to these rumors.[62] One good explanation of this, of course, is to be found in the fact that during the last year or two before the Revolution the Turkish army was honeycombed with minor mutinies directed at squeezing long overdue pay from the government. In any event, the foreign officers were to all intents

[61] "Besonderen Reiz übte auf sie auch der kameradschaftliche Verkehr der fremdländischen Offiziere sowohl innerhalb der eigenen Staatsangehörigkeit als auch zwischen jenen verschiedenen Grossmächte aus, und sie waren ausnahmslos aufrichtig erfreut wenn sie in den ausserdienstlichen Umgang einbezogen wurden." Hubka, "Die Reformaktion, etc.," p. 924. Alfred Rappoport, *Au Pays des Martyrs: Notes et Souvenirs d'un ancien Consul Général d'Autriche-Hongrie en Macédoine (1904-1909)* (Paris, 1927), p. 97, points up the contrast very sharply when he remarks how painful it was for him and Giesl to have high-ranking officers wait on them when they had dinner with Shemsi Pasha, the general who later became one of the few casualties of the Revolution. See also the *Neue Freie Presse* (Vienna), July 21, 1908, p. 2.

[62] Hubka, *Die Oesterreichisch-Ungarische Offiziersmission*, p. 94, notes that "Rittmeister Turić hatte von dort [the vilayet of Kossovo] schon anfangs Juni berichtet, dass Offiziere und aufgeklärte mohammedanische Bürger geheime Besprechungen abhalten, die auf einen Umsturz der bestehenden Staatsordnung gerichtet seien," but there is no evidence that his information attracted any attention in Vienna. According to another contemporary account, a British officer who was "immensely popular with the Turks" knew nothing of the conspiracy until two months before the Revolution, at which time a Turkish officer blurted out to him that events would soon be settled by a "strike of the army." Even then the British officer did not take his Turkish friend seriously. ("The Story of the Young Turks," *Blackwood's Magazine*, CLXXXV [1909], p. 7).

and purposes blind to what their Turkish colleagues were doing.[63]

As far as the common soldier was concerned, life was hard, but then life was always hard. The Turkish peasant was schooled by centuries of hardship to complete indifference and stoicism in the face of conditions which would have caused a mutiny in any other army. He was loyal to his Sultan because he knew no other life and because he held his sovereign in superstitious awe as the fountainhead of authority, both temporal and spiritual. Nationalism was far too remote and incomprehensible an idea to have any meaning to him. Nevertheless, conditions had grown progressively worse under Abdul Hamid, and the common soldier was at least willing to admit that he would prefer to be at home with his family, especially if his period of service had long since been discharged. Like the officer he was rarely paid,[64] his food was poor, his clothing was inadequate, and his general standard of living was little better than that of an animal. He was kept in active service as long as twice the legal period, and it had come to be common knowledge that if he were ordered to some remote outpost of the Empire such as the Yemen, he had little chance of returning.[65]

[63] An examination of such official documentary evidence as is available does not demonstrate that any European officer—with the exception of the case noted in the preceding footnote—warned his government of what was brewing. See for example *Great Britain. Accounts and Papers. 1909*, vol. CV, Cmd. 4529. *Turkey No. 1 (1909). Correspondence respecting the Constitutional Movement in Turkey, 1908*; and Soviet Russia. TSentrarkhiv. A. Popov, "Turetskaia Revolutsiia 1908-1909 gg.," *Krasnyi Arkhiv*, XLIII (1930), pp. 3-54; XLIV (1931), pp. 3-39; XLV (1931), pp. 27-52.

[64] "Pay was constantly in arrear—which explains, if it cannot justify, the terrible looting of villages whose traces I have seen in Macedonia." Buxton, *Turkey in Revolution*, p. 30.

[65] "A friend of mine, who was recently British consul in a Turkish port, after careful investigation in his particular district, found that not more than twenty per cent of the soldiers who were sent to the Yemen returned to their homes." E. F. Knight, *Turkey*, p. 52. Richard Gottheil, "The Young Turks and Old Turkey," *Forum*, XL (December 1908), p. 524, states that between 1903 and the time of the revolution 100,000 Turkish troops lost their lives in the Yemen. See also the story "The Leopard of the Sea," in H. G. Dwight's well-known volume of short stories, *Stamboul Nights* (Garden City, N.Y., 1916).

Thus, while the rank and file of the Turkish army were not actually members of the Society of Union and Progress, their officers, who were, began to prepare them for the Revolution. The Turkish soldier was generally unbelievably ignorant, but he was almost equally credulous if his basic prejudices were avoided. Pashas were too far above him to enter into his comprehension, but he followed his immediate superiors as a child follows his father and accepted what was told him in the same childlike simplicity. It was only necessary for his officers to tell him over and over again that the Sultan was in the hands of corrupt advisers (for the Padishah would never treat his children so shabbily!) and that these advisers must be made away with so that everything would be rosy once more. This groundwork ensured the support of the army when the Revolution did break out, but it also in a measure precluded the dethronement of Abdul Hamid in 1908, for the devotion of the common soldier to the Sultan helped to tie the hands of the officers.

While the Young Turk movement was undergoing its renaissance within the Ottoman Empire, Ahmet Riza, Sabaheddin, and others had kept on with their work, their ranks swelled from time to time by refugees from the despotism of Abdul Hamid. While Sabaheddin was gaining adherents of various nationalities, most Turks were more attracted to the frankly Turkish nationalism of Ahmet Riza's Committee of Union and Progress than to the idealism of Sabaheddin's League of Administrative Decentralization and Private Initiative.

In 1901 two Turks suspected by Yildiz of subversive activities, Sezayi Bey and Dr. Bahaeddin Shakir, fled the country for Paris. The facts are not entirely clear, but they apparently intended to revive the Committee of Union and Progress despite the fact that Ahmet Riza had been carrying on the name since the collapse of the organization in 1897. Eventually, however, they came to an understanding with Ahmet Riza, and an amalgamation of forces resulted at about the time of the 1902 Congress of Ottoman Liberals. Ahmet Riza continued to publish *Mechveret* in French, but a new journal in the Turkish language,

Chourai-Ummet, was launched under the editorship of Sezayi Bey,[66] and the society was considerably enlarged and strengthened. No longer was it merely the struggle of one man and a few associates, and, conversely, no longer was Ahmet Riza the undisputed voice of the society. Both papers continued to make their way into the empire and to find their way into the pockets of the ever-growing group of potential revolutionaries.

The Young Turks of Paris remained in ignorance of the existence of the Ottoman Society of Liberty within the empire until 1907, and the final fusion of the Turkish nationalist groups was effected then only by chance.

In the winter of 1906-1907 the Sultan's spies began to get wind of the fact that something was afoot in Salonika. The size of the revolutionary organization was apparently not suspected, but certain individuals, at least, came under suspicion. In March 1907 Talât (Pasha) came to Ömer Naji and Hüsrev Sami Kızıldoğan, both of whom were, like Talât, members of the Salonika committee, with the information that he had seen secret orders for their arrest.[67] Ömer Naji had brought himself to the attention of Yildiz by engaging in a pen duel with Riza Tevfik in the columns of the Salonika magazine *Çocuk Bahçesi* (*Child's Garden*), a periodical which was shortly thereafter to be banned because of the publication of Mehmet Emin's famous poem "Kayikçi" ("The Boatman"), which subtly depicted the crumbling of the Ottoman Empire under Abdul Hamid.

Ömer Naji and Hüsrev Sami Kızıldoğan immediately set out for Paris, informing only Talât of their plans. Their immediate concern was, of course, to escape arrest, but it was also decided that they should take advantage of their opportunity to study the programs of Ahmet Riza and Sabaheddin with a view to the possibility of joining forces with the one with which they had most in common.[68]

[66] See above, Chapter III.
[67] Kızıldoğan, *op. cit.*, p. 623. Talât, at this time an official in the Salonika post and telegraph administration, saw the ciphered telegram as it came in.
[68] *ibid.*, p. 624.

In the latter part of March the two fugitives reached Paris and commenced their investigation. They soon discovered that the views of the Riza faction were much more closely attuned to the objectives of the Ottoman Society of Liberty than were those of Sabaheddin's group, and they commenced to write un-signed articles for *Chourai-Ummet*.[69] Ömer Naji was particularly welcome in this capacity, for his literary talent had already earned him some notice—apart from the interest taken in him by the Sultan's spies.

Somewhat later that year the union of the two groups was effected "after long conferences and wranglings."[70] Presumably the "wranglings" arose from the difference in outlook between Ahmet Riza and the Ottoman Society of Liberty, for whereas the latter had been formed with one thing in mind—the forcible overturning of the existing government in Turkey—Ahmet Riza had always repudiated the use of violence to achieve the ends he desired. Apparently he was finally persuaded to sacrifice his principles in the interests of unity, for the fusion was accomplished, and he did subsequently subscribe to the program adopted by the second Congress of Ottoman Liberals late in 1907—a program advocating a change of government in the Ottoman Empire by violence if necessary.[71]

Once the two groups had come together, it was decided to adopt the better-known name *İttihat ve Terakki*—Union and Progress—for the entire organization. Dr. Nazim (Selânikli Nazim) was invited by Rahmi Bey to come to Salonika to work with the society within the country. At one of these meetings of the Salonika committee Nazim spoke eloquently of the history of the name *İttihat ve Terakki* and of the sacrifices made under that name, and the committee voted to take the older name in place of their own. Thus, when the revolution broke out in the following year, the organization was operating under the well-known name of the Committee (or Society) of Union and

[69] Letter of Fehmi Janer.   [70] Kızıldoğan, *loc. cit.*
[71] Ahmet Riza yielded very reluctantly, for as late as February 1908 he was giving only qualified support to revolutionary tactics.

Progress—a name adopted out of respect to its predecessors rather than a name acquired by direct inheritance.[72]

The actual fusion of the two groups took place on September 27, 1907. Perhaps "fusion" is not the proper word, however, for the association outlined in the following document:

The "Osmanlı Terakki ve İttihad Society" with its center in Paris and the "Osmanlı Hürriyet Society" with its center in Salonika have united under the name of the "Osmanlı Terakki ve İttihad Cemiyeti" as from 19 Şaban 1325 and 14 September 322 and 27 September 1907[73] with the following stipulations:

Article 1—The society shall have two headquarters, the one being internal and the other external. Of these the external headquarters will be in Paris, and the internal headquarters will be that now located in Salonika, and the two centers will have separate chiefs.

Article 2—The fundamental purpose being to bring into force and continue the constitution of Mithat Pasha published in 1292 [1876], the society, in order to attain this goal will have two separate sets of regulations for at home and abroad, taking into consideration local requirements and tendencies and defining the organization and the duties of individuals.

Article 3—In the realm of financial affairs, the headquarters, no matter how independent, are required to aid one another in case of necessity.

Article 4—The internal headquarters deeming direct communication inadvisable, branches and individuals within the country will, in order to correspond by means of Paris headquarters, be subject to the internal headquarters.

Article 5—The external headquarters will, in addition to being the head office of the branches abroad, fulfil the duty of representing the

[72] Letter of Rahmi Bey, who is at some pains to make it clear that the later Committee of Union and Progress was an entirely different organization from the earlier. Rahmi Bey does not mention the actual fusion of the Salonika and Paris groups but speaks only of making Nazim aware of the Salonika society and inviting him to work with them. Nazim, however, was definitely a member of the directing committee of the Paris group when he went to Salonika and began his work of spreading propaganda in Anatolia.

[73] Three different ways of expressing the same date: the year of the Hejira, the Turkish financial year, a modification of the former which used the solar rather than lunar year and was thus steadily growing apart from the Hejira year, and the Christian date. To add to the complications, the Turkish financial calendar began on March 1, old style. To add still further to the confusion, 322 is a misprint for 323 (1323). The date is given correctly at the end of the document.

society to the outside world. Relations with foreign governments and press are the responsibility of the external headquarters, and the responsibility for internal undertakings and activities is entirely with the internal headquarters.

Article 6—The headquarters are empowered to modify one another's operations only through persuasion.

Article 7—The society's instruments of public dissemination at the moment are the Turkish "Şûrayı Ümmet" and the French "Meşveret" newspapers. Together with aid and support of the internal headquarters in the "Şûrayı Ümmet" published by the foreign headquarters and in all Turkish publications the external headquarters is required to take contributions into consideration and to share the responsibility with the internal headquarters.

> 14 September 1323 1 o'clock *ezani*[74]
> Osmanlı Terakki ve İttihad Cemiyeti
> International and External Affairs Official
> Dr. Bahaeddin [Shakir][75]

Thus was the link forged, but it is perfectly obvious that the Salonika organization intended to pursue its own course and to bring the Paris group in only to the extent of using it to the best possible advantage. Paris was specifically forbidden to meddle in internal affairs. *Mechveret*, Ahmet Riza's private organ, could be left to pursue its own course because it was in French and would have little effect on the people Salonika wanted to reach, but the Turkish language publications were required to accept suggestions from Salonika and in general to give aid and comfort to the cause as seen from that vantage point.

Not long after the above events had taken place, another attempt was made to bring about the fusion of all the groups, Turkish and otherwise, which had in common at least the desire to rid the Ottoman Empire of its hated ruler. In the last days of the year 1907 (December 27-29), a second Congress of Ottoman Liberals met in Paris under the joint presidency of Ahmet Riza, Prince Sabaheddin, and K. Maloumian of the Armenian Revolutionary Federation (Dashnagtzoutian).

---

[74] One hour after sundown by the old Turkish system.
[75] Ahmed Bedevi Kuran, *İnkılâp Tarihimiz ve İttihad ve Terakki*, pp. 238-239.

It would appear that the movement to bring about the Congress of 1907 was instigated by the Armenian Revolutionary Federation, which had recently succeeded in uniting a number of Armenian groups and was now anxious to secure the cooperation of all organizations working in opposition to the existing government in Turkey.[76] In any event, both Turks and Armenians were more disposed to compromise for the sake of unity by this time, and the result was that the delegates to the Congress were actually able to produce a program to which most could adhere. By no means all of the dissatisfied groups of the Empire were represented, however, for Ahmet Riza, in his address to the Congress, deprecated the fact that the "Greek, Albanian, and two Armenian groups are separated from us."[77]

The proceedings of the 1907 Congress do not seem to have been as fully reported as were those of the earlier Congress,[78]

[76] Cf. Dikran Mardiros Bedikian, "The Silent Revolution in Turkey," *The World's Work*, XVI (October 1908), p. 10827, who states that following the amalgamation of the Armenian societies in 1906, Maloumian was commissioned to approach the Turkish societies. Melkon Krischtschian, "Türken und Armenier in Vergangenheit und Gegenwart," *Der Orient*, XI (March-April 1929), p. 73, writes, "Es wird kaum jemand leugnen können, dass die zweimaligen Konferenzen (1903 [*sic*] und 1907) die den Zweck verfolgten, alle ottomanischen Parteien mit der jungtürkischen Bewegung föderative zu verbinden, *auf die armenische Initiative und unermüdliche Arbeit zurückzuführen waren*." (The italics are in the original.) He is, of course, in error about the first congress, which was the work of Damat Mahmut Pasha and his sons.

[77] *Pro-Armenia*, VIII (January 20, 1908), p. 1226. Abraham Galanté, *Turcs et Juifs*, p. 38, gives the following list of organizations which took part in the congress:
"a) Le comité Union et Progrès ottoman. Organes de publication: *Choura-i-Ummet* et *Mechveret*.
b) Les sociétés réunies révolutionnaires arméniennes [Tachnaksoutoun]. Organe de publication: *Trochak*.
c) La société pour l'initiative privée et pour la décentralisation constitutionelle. Organe de publication: *Terreki*.
d) Le comité israélite d'Egypte. Organe de publication: *La Vara*.
e) La rédaction du journal turco-arabe *Hilafet*, publié à Londres.
f) La rédaction du journal *Arménia*, publié à Marseille.
g) La rédaction du journal révolutionnaire *Razmik*, publié dans les pays balkaniques.
h) La rédaction du journal révolutionnaire *Hayrenik*, publié en Amérique.
i) La société *Ahd-i-Osmani*, d'Egypte."
A similar list is to be found in *Pro-Armenia* for January 5, 1908, p. 1215.

[78] Fesch's *Constantinople aux dernières jours d'Abdul-Hamid*, which con-

125

and one is tempted to conclude that this may have been due to a hint that great events were in the making. It is not at all certain that the whole Congress was informed of the widespread organization of the revolutionary society within the Empire, much less that anything in the way of definite plans was divulged. For one thing, it is doubtful if Ahmet Riza was ever kept fully informed of the actual plans for the uprising, which, in any event, were not well developed at this time. Nevertheless, the possibility is strong that the Congress was given at least an inkling of what was afoot. This conclusion is substantiated by the general tenor of the resolutions and decisions of the Congress, which voted, among other things, to set up a permanent secret committee composed of representatives of the organizations which were at work in the interior of the Empire and to keep everything connected with the work of this committee a matter of the strictest secrecy.[79] Another Congress was scheduled to meet in a year's time, but it was provided that in case of an "emergency" the permanent committee could advance the date with the consent of the participating organizations.[80]

The function of the permanent committee was to implement the program adopted by the Congress in every possible way. This program was succinct and to the point: The existing government of the Ottoman Empire must be overthrown and replaced by a representative government, and this must be accomplished by the swiftest possible means, revolutionary or otherwise.[81] The Congress specifically recommended that the

---

tains so full an account of the first congress, was published before the convening of the second.

[79] *Pro-Armenia*, VIII (January 5, 1908), p. 1212. It seems a bit strange that a decision to work in strict secrecy was published at all. It may well be that the whole program was supposed to be kept secret, for Ahmet Riza subsequently scored the Armenians for being in such a hurry to communicate the program to the press. (See below.) However, Angus Hamilton, *Problems of the Middle East* (London, 1909), p. 27, states that at the conclusion of the congress "Young Turk organs" openly referred to the success they had been having with the army, thereby putting the Sultan on guard.

[80] *Pro-Armenia, loc. cit.*

[81] *idem*; see also Abraham Galanté, *loc. cit.*

Turkish government be opposed in every possible way, and a list of suggested forms of opposition was made. These included: 1) armed resistance to acts of oppression; 2) unarmed resistance in the form of political and economic strikes, including strikes by government officials and the police; 3) passive resistance in the form of refusal to pay taxes; 4) the circulation of propaganda in the army—propaganda inviting the soldiers to refuse to march against the people or against revolutionary groups; 5) general insurrection if necessary; 6) such other means of action as might be imposed by circumstances.[82]

The above recommendations demonstrate that the Turkish organizations were prepared to accept the tactics long since adopted by the Armenian societies, tactics very similar to those the radical groups tried to use in the last stages of the Russian Revolution of 1905. Sabaheddin had long been working with the Armenians, but it is very doubtful that Ahmet Riza would have subscribed to such a program had he not known of the existence of the underground movement in Macedonia—and he subscribed with reluctance as it was. A month after the Congress adjourned he antagonized the Armenians once more by publishing in *Mechveret*, under the title "Prudence et Modestie," an article taking the Armenians to task for crowing about their success in securing general support of their tactics, tactics which they boasted were "proven by experience."[83] This reference to the earlier work of the Armenian societies was too much for Ahmet Riza's Turkish nationalism. He reproached the Armenians for being the first to communicate the decisions of the Congress to the press and for making out that the Turks had become "terrorists." We will not, he declared, adopt the revolutionary tactics employed "without success" by "certain Armenians." "We are met," he continued, "not to commit follies and crimes or to create a pretext for the intervention of the Powers, but to realize a noble aim . . . by revolutionary means which

[82] *Pro-Armenia, loc. cit.*
[83] *Pro-Armenia,* pp. 1241-1242, quoting *Mechveret* of February 1, 1908.

suit the temper of our compatriots."[84] *Pro-Armenia* countered by pointing out that Ahmet Riza had, on behalf of the Committee of Union and Progress, signed his name to resolutions which were in complete opposition to the "expectative" tactics he advocated.[85]

It is worth noting that the issue on which the first Congress had foundered, the question of foreign intervention, does not figure at all in the reported findings of the 1907 Congress. Either the Armenians (and Sabaheddin) were more disposed to compromise this time, or they had finally realized that it was useless to expect the powers to take wholehearted and thoroughgoing action.

The fact that agreement was reached on the surface at the 1907 Congress does not mean that the basic disparities of view among the various anti-Hamidian factions were by any means resolved. Actually, by 1907 the gap between the partisans of Ahmet Riza and the followers of Sabaheddin had grown so great as to be completely irreconcilable, a fact which was to have its greatest significance after the Revolution.[86]

Both Ahmet Riza and Sabaheddin made addresses to the Congress which demonstrated clearly that each was still cleaving to his own line. Ahmet Riza was moderate, to be sure, but his Positivism cropped out once more when he made an appeal for solidarity in the interests of "the great majority who aspire to a reign of order and progress."[87] Sabaheddin delivered himself

---

[84] *idem.*   [85] *Pro-Armenia*, pp. 1241-1242.

[86] Ahmed Bedevi Kuran, *İnkılâp Tarihimiz ve İttihad ve Terakki*, pp. 228-229, prints a letter of June 11, 1907 from Dr. Bahaeddin Shakir to an unnamed person in Constantinople who had inquired why the Committee of Union and Progress was so bitterly opposed to Sabaheddin. In the letter Sabaheddin and his father are accused of having left Constantinople to "rob the public treasure and to sell the country to foreign powers." Sabaheddin is further accused of consorting with Armenian revolutionaries and of desiring to establish an Armenian state within the Ottoman Empire. Ahmet Riza, on the other hand, is described as an "honest and patriotic man." I am in complete agreement with Kuran that the charges of venality leveled against Sabaheddin are false; the letter is mentioned only in order to demonstrate the intensity of the feeling which prevailed.

[87] *Pro-Armenia*, p. 1226.

of a long peroration heavily larded with quotations from Demolins. Turkey he compared to the South American countries, where, he declared (after Demolins), the individual repulsed effort and initiative with the result that the state interfered tyrannically in private life. History, he declaimed, shows us that the greatest and strongest people in the world have been those who have dealt as little as possible with politics.[88]

Actually, neither Ahmet Riza nor Sabaheddin need have wasted his breath, however, for neither their addresses nor anything else that was said at the Congress of 1907 had any effect on the Young Turk Revolution. Decisions were now being made within the empire, and the new organization which now bore the old name, "Committee of Union and Progress," concerned itself very little with the Young Turks of Paris. The reconciliation with the Armenian Revolutionary Federation sounded imposing, for example, but it remained completely on the theoretical level. That is to say, the Dashnagtzoutian and other Armenian groups were active in fomenting dissatisfaction both before and after the Congress of 1907, but they never worked in conjunction with the Committee of Union and Progress, which indeed, had little or no sympathy for the aspirations of any of the minority groups of the Ottoman Empire.[89]

Here it must be emphasized, then, that there was never a real coordination between the groups within and without the empire. Ahmet Riza, even after the adoption by the Turkish revolutionary group of the name of his organization, had no direct influence on the course of events. It is true that he was subsequently elected to the presidency of the new Turkish Chamber, but this was only in recognition of his relentless fight against the régime—and because his philosophy was so closely akin to that of the men who actually carried out the revolution.

[88] idem.
[89] The letters of Dr. Ali Osman Onbulak, Fehmi Janer, and Dr. Akil Muhtar Özden all emphasize the fact that the only connection between the Committee of Union and Progress and other revolutionary organizations was through the Paris congresses and that there was no contact between them inside the Ottoman Empire.

Even then he was not particularly important in Young Turk circles, for the real power lay with the men who remained behind the scenes.[90]

Toward the end of 1906 a series of mutinies broke out in the Turkish army in various parts of the country, the most serious disturbances being in the more remote parts of Anatolia. Most of the mutinies were little more than strikes to force the distribution of long-overdue pay, and the number of these strikes increased as it was discovered that gratifying results could be obtained by this method. Troops had never been paid regularly under Abdul Hamid, yet never before had there been anything quite on the scale of this wave of mutinies and demonstrations. One of the revolts took place among troops which had received orders to embark for the Yemen, for, despite its name, this area was anything but fortunate for the Turkish soldiers stationed there.

In 1907 the number of mutinies increased still more,[91] and, during the course of the year, civilians began to participate in Anatolia. Uprisings against corrupt officials took place in Bitlis, Van, Erzurum, and other cities. Governors were deposed and new laws rejected by popular movements which the army made no attempt to suppress. And the army mutinies now commenced to spread. In October 1907 there was trouble in Constantinople itself, and at the beginning of 1908 the ferment spread to Smyrna and even down into Syria.

These mutinies were by no means confined to the common soldier. Officers joined the men in demands for back pay, and the officers had a grievance of their own: it was almost impossible to advance in rank on the basis of merit and service alone.

[90] "Once, about the middle of December, 1916, Enver even went so far as to hurl the epithet 'shameless dog' at Ahmed Riza in the Senate. . . ." Dr. Harry Stuermer, *Two War Years in Constantinople: Sketches of German and Young Turkish Ethics and Politics* (New York, 1917), p. 256.

[91] The *Neue Freie Presse* of Vienna reported on July 23, 1908, that "*in the preceding year in all corps-areas seventeen larger mutinies and revolts of whole troop-units or garrisons* took place, of which most lasted several days, countless smaller mutinies and demonstrations not counted." The italics are in the original.

Most of the demands made by the army were met, for Abdul Hamid dared not allow it to get completely out of hand. The myth of Abdul Hamid's astuteness is nowhere more completely disproved than in his relationship with his army, which he allowed to crumble to pieces and then tried to patch up when it was far too late.

Thus Abdul Hamid was beginning to reap the fruits of his misrule. Part of the ferment was due to the fact that 1907 was a year of economic crisis in the Ottoman Empire, but there can be no question but that the Young Turk propaganda was beginning to take effect and to make use of the discontent of people and army alike. For years Abdul Hamid had been filling Anatolia with political exiles, and these men in particular helped greatly to undermine the government.

Sabaheddin's League of Administrative Decentralization and Private Initiative seems to have been concentrating on spreading propaganda in Asia Minor in conjunction with the Armenian groups, but it is doubtful if their program was well-developed or very far advanced when the Revolution broke out. Nevertheless, their propaganda was meeting with increasing success along the same lines as those which were laid down as the program of the Congress of 1907.

A certain amount of propaganda work in units of the Turkish army stationed in the Smyrna area and other parts of Asia Minor was undertaken by the Committee of Union and Progress from Salonika, but no attempt was made to extend the organization itself to Anatolia on anything like the scale on which it operated in Macedonia. Particularly active in this work was Selânikli Nazim, who wandered through the country in a variety of disguises, sowing dissatisfaction as he went, for more than a year before the outbreak of the Revolution. He eventually had the satisfaction of knowing that his work (and the work of others) had been successful, for the troops from Asia Minor fraternized with those of Macedonia when Abdul Hamid made one last attempt to forestall the movement by shipping troops to Salonika from Smyrna.

In July of 1908 the Young Turk Revolution finally broke out "like a crash of innocuous thunder."[92] There was nothing to distinguish it at first from the mutinies which had become so commonplace in the preceding year. Most contemporary observers of the Turkish scene attached little importance to the news that there was a renewed outbreak of trouble in the Third Army Corps in Macedonia, even though occasional outbursts of violence marred what had come to be accepted as the established pattern.

But at Yildiz Saray it had finally begun to be understood some time before the events of July that something more ominous than than local manifestations of the current "sit-down strike" problem was afoot. The broad hints emanating from the 1907 Congress of Ottoman Liberals possibly had something to do with the arousing of suspicions, as was noted above, and the very size of the Committee of Union and Progress precluded its remaining forever undetected in an empire so infested with spies as that of Abdul Hamid. Only the fact that the society was as well organized as it was had kept it from being ferreted out before. Thus, while it does not appear that there was a single case of outright betrayal,[93] it was only a matter of time until the Sultan's spies would nose out some information about the organization.

Late in the spring of 1908 a commission was finally sent to Salonika to conduct a thorough investigation into the rumors and reports which were beginning to mount up. It seems likely that the palace had, over a period of years, become so used to the staggering volume of "jurnals" or reports submitted by its spies that when the reports finally began to mean something, the spies found themselves in the position of the boy who had cried "wolf!" too often. That is to say, when the first commission was sent to Salonika, it was already too late. On June 11, Nazim

[92] Aubrey Herbert, *Ben Kendim: A Record of Eastern Travel* (2nd edn.; London: n.d.), p. 257.
[93] Cf. Knight, *Turkey*, p. 109: "There was not one single instance of the betrayal of his brethren by a member of the society." Buxton, *Turkey in Revolution*, p. 48, states "There is no proof of a single betrayal by any initiated member."

Bey, who had been appointed military commandant of Salonika for the purpose of conducting the investigation, was shot and wounded as he was leaving for Constantinople to make his report. Now thoroughly alarmed, the palace immediately dispatched another commission under Ismail Mahir Pasha.

In view of the attention which was beginning to be concentrated upon them, the Committee of Union and Progress began to stir uneasily. It is impossible to ascertain if a definite date had been set for the projected revolution, but it is possible to say that the uprising was not scheduled to commence when it did.[94] But the fact that the Sultan was beginning to take alarm, plus the fact that the international situation was, from the standpoint of the intensely nationalistic young officers who composed the greatest part of the society, growing daily more ominous, eventually precipitated the revolt in the summer of 1908.

The latter factor—that is, the international situation—has probably been somewhat overemphasized as an immediate cause of the Young Turk Revolution. It is true that the Reval meeting between Edward VII and Nicholas II on June 9 and 10, 1908, did cause some concern to the Committee of Union and Progress, for the fear was widespread that England was pre-

[94] It would seem likely that the uprising had been planned by the Salonika committee to begin in the fall of 1908. Richard Gottheil, "The Young Turks and Old Turkey," *Forum*, XL (December 1908), p. 525, says, "There seems to be little doubt that the general uprising was planned to take place in Macedonia on September 1, 1908 and that much blood was expected to flow before the Sultan would be made to come to heel." Buxton, *op. cit.*, p. 53, states, "The date of the intended rising was fixed for the feast of Bairam, in the coming autumn of 1908." On the other hand, Knight, who set out to write a history of the Revolution shortly after it had taken place, writes (*op. cit.*, p. 118), "It had been calculated by the Young Turks that the time would not be ripe for their great *coup* until the autumn of 1909, but the menace of further foreign intervention in Macedonia and the active campaign against the Committee, which was opened by the Palace at the beginning of 1908, precipitated the revolt." In connection with Knight's book, it must be noted that his chronology is completely untrustworthy even on events which had already taken place and were not in the realm of speculation. Finally, Wilfred T. F. Castle states in his *Grand Turk* (London, New York, Melbourne, 1943 [?]), p. 74, that the day had been fixed for August 31, 1908, the anniversary of Abdul Hamid's accession to the throne. However, Castle's book is hardly a scholarly work, and he cites no authority for the above statement.

paring to abandon her traditional opposition to Russian ambitions in the Near East and that this might well mean the end of Turkish rule in Macedonia and perhaps in all of Turkey in Europe.[95] This apprehension was undoubtedly strengthened by the news that the Russian fleet was conducting "routine maneuvers" off the Turkish Black Sea coast a few days later.[96]

The immediate impetus to the Revolution was almost undoubtedly given, however, by the necessity for acting before the Sultan moved to break up the conspiracy. The Reval meeting coincided with the first outbreak of violence and may have given just the added fillip that was needed to set things in motion, but the attempt on the life of Nazim Bey on June 11 was made to prevent him from getting back to Constantinople with the results of an investigation launched well before the Reval meeting. On June 19 Sami Bey, Inspector of Police in Krushevo, was severely wounded, and then things began to happen in rapid succession. Ismail Mahir Pasha's commission began to get closer and closer to an understanding of the true state of affairs, and a number of officers were arrested and sent to Constantinople for interrogation.

At the end of June a young officer named Enver Bey, a member of the Committee of Union and Progress but not at the time any more important than the average young officer who had become affiliated with the society, decided that it would be more expedient to disappear into the hills than to accept an invitation to visit Constantinople and accept a promotion in rank. His disappearance produced a mild flurry of excitement, and the *Frankfurter Zeitung's* correspondent in Salonika reported, "It is feared that he is the victim of Young Turks."[97]

A few days later, on July 4, another officer, Niyazi Bey, took

[95] Cf. the "Annual Report for 1908" of the British Ambassador at Constantinople (at this time Sir Gerard Lowther, who arrived at his new post on July 30, 1908) in *British Documents on the Origins of the War, 1898-1914*, vol. v, p. 249. Such a prognostication was not far wrong, for England by this time was reaching the conclusion that she had nothing to lose in Turkey, where her influence was at its lowest ebb.

[96] See the *Neue Freie Presse* (Vienna), June 20, 1908.

[97] As quoted in the *Neue Freie Presse* for July 2, 1908.

to the hills for similar reasons, but his motives for departing were not in doubt for a moment, for he took with him a large number of followers and helped himself to a quantity of arms, ammunition, and money from the stores of his company as he departed.[98] Niyazi was soon joined by another young officer, Eyüp Sabri, but there was still no general uprising.

In point of fact, there was never anything like an order from Salonika for the Revolution to begin. The uprising simply developed spontaneously as the news spread from one unit to another, for the various Young Turk committees of Macedonia did not consider themselves to be under the orders of Salonika. Ömer Fevzi Mardin, who, at the time of the Revolution, commanded the gendarmerie post at Gevgeli, north of Salonika, states categorically that the local committee in his area made its own decision about declaring for the constitution and that the influence of Salonika was purely a moral one.[99] It seems likely, however, that had the Revolution not been precipitated when it was, the Salonika committee would have been able to obtain agreement from the other centers on some definite date. Charles Roden Buxton, writing soon after the Revolution, summed up the relationship among the various groups very well when he said: "There seems to have been, in the working of this widespread association of isolated units, a complete though half-unconscious cooperation."[100]

The story of the final stages of the Revolution is too well known to require a detailed narrative here. Suffice it to say that after Shemsi Pasha, who had been entrusted by the Sultan with the task of putting down the mutinies in Macedonia, was shot down in broad daylight in the streets of Monastir on July 7, one unit of the Third Army Corps after another came out into

[98] Buxton, *op. cit.*, p. 57; the *Neue Freie Presse* reported the incident on July 8, 1908, but was unable to see in it anything more than a purely local disturbance and saw fit to point out to its readers that all reports of Young Turk activity must be treated with great caution, for the Turkish army in general had far too much respect for the Sultan as head of the army ever to revolt against him.
[99] Letter of Ömer Fevzi Mardin.
[100] Buxton, *op. cit.*, p. 48.

the open and declared for the constitution. Troops were hurriedly dispatched from Asia Minor, but they were already partly infected, and further propaganda work aboard the vessels during the voyage from Smyrna to Salonika rendered them completely useless to the Sultan. Decorations, promotions, and back pay were showered on Army and Navy officers, but it was too late for such measures. The Albanians, on whom Abdul Hamid had always leaned very heavily, were in a state of unrest and joined in the demands for the restoration of the constitution.

On July 24 Abdul Hamid, by now seriously alarmed for his own safety, which was, after all, the sole and entire preoccupation of the Hamidian system, bowed to the inevitable and announced to his people that the constitution of 1876, which he had so zealously been preserving until such time as it could be of use,[101] was now in effect once more.[102] The Revolution was over, and it had succeeded beyond the wildest dreams of the

[101] Gotthard Jäschke, "Die Entwicklung des osmanischen Verfassungsstaates von den Anfängen bis zur Gegenwart," *Die Welt des Islams*, v (1917), p. 19, points out that the constitution was never formally repealed and was published regularly every year in the government year-book.

[102] According to legend, the momentous decision was finally made by the Sultan only after he had been advised to do so by his astrologer, Ebül Huda. The ingenious thesis has also been advanced that Abdul Hamid really welcomed the Young Turk revolution because he "preferred to surrender to a New Turkey, young and vibrant, than to perish in the ruins of his Empire." (Wade Dewood David, *European Diplomacy in the Near Eastern Question 1906-1909* [Urbana, Illinois, 1940], p. 64). David cites in support of this idea the memoirs of Tahsin Pasha, Abdul Hamid's chamberlain (Tahsin Paşa, *Abdülhamit ve Yıldız Hatıraları* [İstanbul, 1931], p. 293). Tahsin Pasha does remark that Reval brought matters to a head, and he also says, as he looks back, "Had the revolution of 1324 [1908] not taken place like a heavenly miracle the Turks would have found themselves forced from the soil of Europe even at this time." Nowhere, however, does he indicate that Abdul Hamid welcomed the revolution, even as the lesser of two evils. David's other citations, moreover, are confused and vague and offer no substantiation of his contention, and his quotation from Giesl's *Zwei Jahrzehnte im Nahen Orient* (from p. 187 rather than p. 87 as David indicates) is a complete mistranslation and a complete misunderstanding of what is being discussed. C. H. Becker, *Islamstudien*, II, p. 351, does note that the first reaction of French diplomats was that the Revolution was a coup de théâtre staged by the Young Turks and Abdul Hamid together in view of the international situation but that this hypothesis was soon abandoned. My own view is that Abdul Hamid gave in reluctantly in order to save his throne—an attempt in which he was, unfortunately, successful.

Young Turks, for it had been accomplished virtually without bloodshed.

The whole of the Ottoman Empire went wild with joy. In the oft-quoted words of William Miller,[103]

> For some days Macedonia seemed to have become Utopia. Enver Bey exclaimed that 'arbitrary government' had 'disappeared.' 'Henceforth,' cried this enthusiastic leader of the revolution, 'we are all brothers. There are no longer Bulgars, Greeks, Roumans, Jews, Mussulmans; under the same blue sky we are all equal, we glory in being Ottomans.' At Serres the president of the Bulgarian Committee embraced the Greek Archbishop; at Drama the revolutionary officers imprisoned a Turk for insulting a Christian; in an Armenian cemetery a procession of Turks and Armenians listened to prayers, offered up by their respective priests, for the victims of the Armenian massacres; at Samsun the Turks saluted the beard of a Greek prelate; at Tripoli Turks and Arabs joined in thanksgiving services. The Bulgarian bands surrendered, and the brigand Sandanski was received like the prodigal son.

The Ottoman Empire was, then, a constitutional state once more, and for nearly a year Abdul Hamid played what for him was a very strange and most unwelcome role—that of constitutional monarch. The very fact that he retained the throne has occasioned much speculation and some suspicion of the sincerity of the Young Turks of 1908. The deposition of Abdul Hamid was, after all, the objective towards which the Young Turks had been working for many years; it was the one aim which all parties and factions enjoyed in common; and it was constantly put forward as the panacea which would, at a stroke, solve all the problems of the moribund Ottoman Empire.

The reason for the retention of Abdul Hamid on the throne is to be found in the simple fact that the Committee of Union and Progress did not feel strong enough to force the issue in 1908. The Sultan had stolen their thunder to some extent by giving in to the demands for the restoration of the constitution

[103] *The Ottoman Empire and its Successors, 1801-1927, with an Appendix, 1927-1936* (Cambridge, 1936), p. 476. I have encountered this quotation in many a book on Turkey, but very few have been thoughtful enough to attribute it to its author.

and had even been fairly successful in making it appear that the idea was his own. Moreover, despite his years of misrule, he still commanded the blind veneration of the vast, ignorant majority of the Turkish people—or rather, the exalted position which he occupied still blinded the Turkish people to his real character. The Committee of Union and Progress was almost wholly made up of officers, the intelligentsia of Turkey, but for the execution of their program they were forced to depend on the rank and file of the army, which consisted of a cross section of the Turkish people. As has already been noted,[104] the Committee of Union and Progress had not dared to direct its propaganda among the common soldiers against the Sultan himself, for in the army the Sultan was revered not only because of his position as the head of a theocratic state but also because of the traditional role of the Turkish Sultans as commanders of the army in a military state.

In the first few days after the restoration of the constitution the Committee of Union and Progress became acutely aware of the intensity of this feeling when officers of the Third Army Corps arrived in Adrianople and attempted to turn the men against the Sultan. The British Consul in that city reported the first phase of the incident in the following words:[105]

Yesterday afternoon a deputation of six officers from the IIIrd Army Corps arrived here by special train. . . . Shouts of "Long live the Sultan" were raised by the crowd, who were thereupon addressed by an officer requesting them to cease shouts of this nature, since the Constitution had not been granted by the Sultan, but extorted from him by the efforts of the Committee.

The officers then proceeded to pull down all inscriptions of "Long live the Sultan!" many of which were displayed at the station. This action was apparently entirely approved of by the soldiers. I understand that the officers consider this to have been the crucial point of the day's proceedings, since although the rank and file had sworn allegiance to the Committee on the 26th instant they were uncertain how this action might be regarded by them.

[104] *supra*, Chapter IV.
[105] Consul Samson to Mr. G. Barclay, Adrianople, July 29, 1908, *Turkey No. 1* (1909), p. 985.

But the officers were soon disabused of their belief that the crisis had passed. The new British Ambassador, Sir Gerard Lowther, reported to London on August 4 concerning the situation in Adrianople:[106]

On the 1st August . . . a violent reaction set in against the strong feeling that had found expression on the evening of the 28th July. The troops rose against their officers, declaring they believed it was their aim to kill or dethrone the Sultan. . . .

The soldiery insisted on sending a delegation composed of some 350 of their number to Constantinople to assure the Sultan of their loyalty, and to satisfy themselves that he was alive and safe.

In Constantinople itself the Committee was particularly weak, for in that city little had been done since the debacle of 1897 had destroyed the spirit of the movement. This factor was also important in influencing the decision of the Committee not to press the issue,[107] but my Turkish informants are virtually unanimously agreed that Abdul Hamid had to be left on the throne in 1908 simply because the Committee of Union and Progress did not feel that they could afford to prejudice the gains they had made by precipitating the question of deposing the Sultan.[108] The experience with the Turkish common soldier in Adrianople gave them some idea of what might happen if Abdul Hamid determined to appeal to the fanaticism of the Turkish people. Much bloodletting would inevitably have resulted, and the issue might have gone against them. However, the failure to depose the Sultan did not mean that the Committee of Union and Progress had forgotten the misrule of Abdul Hamid or that they at any time gave credence to his professions of satisfaction with the new régime.[109] The fact that they did not trust him is amply demonstrated by the fact that the seat of the Committee of Union and Progress remained at Salonika.

[106] Sir G. Lowther to Sir Edward Grey, Therapia, August 4, 1908, *ibid.*, p. 995.
[107] Letter of Dr. Akil Muhtar Özden.
[108] Letters of Dr. Ali Osman Onbulak, Ömer Fevzi Mardin, Fehmi Janer.
[109] "The directors of Union and Progress at no time believed in the sincerity of Abdülhamit. This point is definite." Letter of Fehmi Janer. See also Salih Keramett Bey, "The Young Turk Movement," in Eliot Grinnell Mears, *Modern Turkey* (New York, 1924), p. 487.

CHAPTER V

Conclusions—The Failure to Depose Abdul Hamid—The Role of the Great Powers—Epilogue

AN EXAMINATION of the results of the Young Turk Revolution, either internally or externally, is not within the province of this study, but an analysis of the origins of the Revolution would not be complete without some discussion of the possibility of outside influences on the Revolution. It has been suggested, for example, that the Revolution of 1908 was instigated by Germany, the grounds for this belief being found in the fact that within a very short time after the Revolution, German influence was paramount in Turkey. This thesis disregards the fact that German influence was paramount before the Revolution and that there was no reason to risk what was already a highly satisfactory situation.

To go back a bit, it must be noted that Abdul Hamid's hit-or-miss foreign policy had gradually come to have one or two cardinal points. By the beginning of the century he had come to look upon Germany as virtually the only nation friendly to Turkey—or, to put it as Abdul Hamid would have done, to him. Of great importance were the visits of the German Emperor in 1888 and 1898, the last coming at a time when no other sovereign would have sullied himself by visiting the "Red Sultan." Germany consistently followed a policy of avoiding any action which might give offense to the Sultan, abstaining, for example, from the occasional naval demonstrations by means of which the other powers imposed their wills on Abdul Hamid. The Sultan was aware of the fact that the Germans were playing a shrewd game for their own advantage, but he used to say of them, "The Germans do me as much good as they are permitted to do, whereas the rest of Europe do me as much harm as they can."[1]

[1] Arminius Vambéry, "Personal Recollections of Abdul Hamid and his Court," *Nineteenth Century*, LXVI (July 1909), p. 81.

At the other extreme of influence in 1908 was England, the traditional defender of the inviolability of the Ottoman Empire. Abdul Hamid was fanatical in his hatred of the English, to whom he ascribed most of his difficulties with the minorities of the empire. Because of the change in Anglo-Turkish relationships during the reign of Abdul Hamid, England gradually dropped her old role as the protector of the Sick Man. Salisbury was prepared as early as 1895 to precipitate the splitting up of the Ottoman Empire but was unable to convince the other powers of England's disinterestedness even though he was ready to accede to Russian aspirations.[2] A few years later Grey lent a willing ear to Izvolskii's plaintive request for consideration of Russia's urge to the sea. Not until after the Revolution of 1908 did England revert to her old position—at least temporarily—for, until the Revolution shackled Abdul Hamid, England had no hope of improving her position in Turkey.

Of the other major powers, Russia enjoyed the best reputation with the Sultan. After the Congress of Berlin Russia had temporarily shelved her aspirations with regard to the straits. A personal relationship of a sort had existed between Alexander III and Abdul Hamid,[3] and it appears that the Sultan admired the autocratic ways of the Tsars.[4] In any event, Russia was not pressing hard to obtain a favorable solution of the Near Eastern question during the greater part of the reign of Abdul Hamid. Her eyes were turned to the Far East, and, in general, she was content to maintain the status quo in the Near East during the period between the Congress of Berlin and the Russo-Japanese war. In any event, the known anti-Russian attitude of

[2] William L. Langer, *The Diplomacy of Imperialism* (New York, 1935), vol. I, pp. 195ff.

[3] Vambéry, *loc. cit.*

[4] "I have heard on good authority that when the Sultan's officers congratulated him on the defeat of his old enemy Russia [in 1905], he replied that he did not by any means consider the result of the war a matter of congratulation, because he and the Czar were the only autocratic monarchs in Europe, and the defeat of the Czar meant a blow to the principle of autocracy." Sir Charles Eliot, *Turkey in Europe* (new edn.; London, 1908), p. 426.

the Young Turks meant that Russian influence would inevitably be lessened if the Young Turks came into power.

Austria-Hungary was cordially disliked by the Sultan, but he counted on his German friends to keep her in line. The Dual Monarchy was plagued by internal difficulties as well and was consequently anxious to keep the Near Eastern situation from coming to a head. To that end she had concluded an agreement with Russia in 1897 which left both powers free to turn their attention elsewhere. In this agreement both powers agreed to maintain the existing situation in the Near East as long as possible. Like Russia, Austria-Hungary had nothing to gain by a strengthening of the Ottoman Empire, and Aehrenthal's seizure of Bosnia-Herzegovina shortly after the Revolution demonstrates his fear that the Young Turk government would become so much stronger than that of Abdul Hamid that soon it might be more difficult to annex these provinces.

France had many interests in the Ottoman Empire. She was interested in maintaining the empire because of her large investments in that area, although she often found herself forced to put pressure on the Sultan's government, either alone or in conjunction with other powers, because of these investments and because of her traditional role as protector of the Catholics in the Ottoman Empire. But a solution of the Near Eastern question along lines which would lessen the influence of Germany without impairing French interests would have been welcome; so that it may be said that France had no overwhelming·desire to see the status quo preserved forever beyond the traditional inclination of most of the powers to procrastinate rather than face the problems which would inevitably be raised by any change in the situation.

As for Italy, the sixth great power in 1908, there can be little question but that she felt that the status quo served her well enough until such time as the break-up of the empire did come about. She had her eye on Tripolitania, but, as Giolitti remarks in his memoirs,[5]

[5] Giovanni Giolitti, *Memoirs of My Life* (London, 1923), p. 251.

It was not necessary to have recourse to military measures to solve the Libyan question during the reign of Abdul Hamid, from whom we could obtain concessions of an economic and legal character such as would have ensured Italian interests against any other aims at expansion.

From the foregoing it may be seen that England was by far the most logical candidate for the honor of overthrowing Abdul Hamid, for England had reached the point where she had nothing to lose by upsetting the existing order in the Ottoman Empire. All of the other powers, with the exception of Germany, had territorial ambitions in the Near East, but for various reasons most of them were still more afraid of precipitating trouble than of realizing these ambitions. Moreover, England was the only power, with the possible exception of France, which could contemplate without fear the establishment of a stronger government in Turkey.

It would not be surprising to discover, then, that England had supported the Young Turk movement. However, the conclusion to which one is forced after a study of the origins of the Revolution is that no foreign power supported the Young Turks or even had any advance knowledge of the Revolution. This conclusion is supported by a number of factors.

In the first place, it must be borne in mind that the Young Turks of 1908, the Committee of Union and Progress, were unalterably opposed to foreign intervention in the affairs of the Ottoman Empire and that one of the factors which gave the Revolution its initial impetus was the fear of further foreign intervention.

It is perhaps from a misunderstanding of exactly who the men who actually made the Revolution were that some of the speculation about the possibilities of foreign influence on the Revolution has arisen. It has been pointed out that Ahmet Riza was a Positivist, and it has been alleged that Sabaheddin was under the influence of French Catholicism and even of the House of Orléans.[6] But to suggest from such facts and allegations that the

---

[6] On the latter point see especially the discussion in Chapter III, above.

Young Turk Revolution was French-inspired or promoted by either the Positivists or the Catholic church is even more ridiculous than the far more widespread assertion that the Revolution was a product of international Freemasonry.[7] In the last analysis the Young Turks of Paris and other European centers had little or no direct influence on the Revolution when it did break out. Sabaheddin was not a member of the Committee of Union and Progress, and even Ahmet Riza, as we have already seen, was largely ignored by the society operating inside the empire.

But the most convincing proof that the Young Turk Revolution was not furthered by outside influences is to be found in the complete absence of satisfactory evidence to the contrary. As an anonymous writer[8] noted a few weeks after the outbreak of the revolution,

Almost more extraordinary than the sudden and irresistible sweep of the revolution itself was the total absence of pre-vision with regard to it. For years masses of literature, official and otherwise, have been heaped together in every language. There have been Blue-books, Yellow-books, Green-books, and other books, an unending succession of volumes in all the colours of the spectrum. Not a single word can apparently be found in these compilations which could be taken as foreshadowing the possibility of what has occurred. Baron Marschall, in Constantinople, is one of the ablest and most experienced figures in the diplomatic service of any nation, but it is clear that the Wilhelmstrasse was as much surprised as the Foreign Office of any other nation.

Time has justified the assertion of the writer quoted above. In none of the great documentary collections published by the various European governments after World War I can one find so much as a hint that any cabinet had foreknowledge of the Young Turk Revolution, much less that any country was encouraging the revolutionists. On July 10, 1908, two weeks before the proclamation of constitutional government in Turkey, the German representative in Constantinople, Kiderlen-Waechter, reported to his government that

[7] On the Freemasonic question see Chapter IV, above.
[8] "Viator," "The Turkish Revolution," *Fortnightly Review*, XC (September 1908), pp. 357-358.

Under "Young Turks" can be included, according to the current conception, those people who, filled, perhaps more infected, with Western European notions without deeper knowledge, dream of a "Reformation" of their fatherland through the introduction of so-called parliamentary institutions after some European pattern. I scarcely believe that these enthusiasts are very numerous, even less that they are directly dangerous.[9]

One of the German Emperor's famous marginal annotations has been quoted as evidence that the Revolution was German-inspired:

The Revolution was made, not by the "Young Turks" from Paris and London, but alone by the army and as a matter of fact exclusively by the so-called "German officers" educated in Germany. A purely military revolution. These officers have things under control and are absolutely Germanophile [Deutschgesonnen].[10]

However, it is clear that what the Kaiser meant when he said that the Young Turks were "Deutschgesonnen" was that he was confident that German training had made the officers who played a leading role in the Revolution sympathetic to Germany.[11] This was a shrewd prognostication, and there can be no doubt that the Kaiser was well informed on the situation after the Revolution took place, although he was incorrect in assuming that the "German officers" were solely responsible for the Revolution. The most pro-German of them all, Enver Bey, was only thrown to the top by the circumstances of the moment.

In the case of England the absence of advance knowledge is just as apparent. Sir Gerard Lowther, the new British ambassador to Turkey, was actually en route to his new post when the Revolution took place, and was hailed deliriously by vast crowds

---

[9] *Die Grosse Politik der Europäischen Kabinette, 1871-1914*, vol. XXV:2, No. 8875, The Acting Ambassador in Constantinople von Kiderlen to the Chancellor Prince von Bülow, 10 July, 1908. See also Ernst Jäckh (ed.), *Kiderlen-Wächter, der Staatsmann und Mensch: Briefwechsel und Nachlass* (Berlin & Leipzig, 1925), vol. I, pp. 267ff. for further evidence of the fact that Kiderlen was completely unaware of what was about to happen.

[10] *Grosse Politik*, XXV:2, No. 8906, minute of the Kaiser on a memorandum of Count von Metternich dated August 14, 1908.

[11] Dr. Ernst Jäckh, who was in a position to know, agreed entirely with this interpretation in a personal letter dated February 5, 1941.

on his arrival. One of the rumors which was current for a time in the streets of Constantinople was that the constitution was the gift of the English nation,[12] but, as Sir Edward Grey wrote to Sir Gerard on July 31, "How little either of us foresaw, when you were appointed, the reception you would actually get!"[13]

Aside from the evidence—or rather, lack of evidence—in the available documentary collections,[14] Turkish sources are unanimous in denying the existence of support of the movement or even of foreknowledge on the part of any foreign power. Riza Tevfik Bey writes, for example:

> All the Embassies at Stamboul were unpleasantly amazed of the sudden outburst of the Revolution. They were not expecting it at all; it was intempestive. I was then an important member of the central Committee, responsible for controlling the Capital and keeping it in Order. I had a young officer with me; we were leading the crowd in the manifestations made before the Embassies. We had been very coldly received. You know the attitude of Austria-Hungary and Bulgaria, just after the proclamation of the constitution, certainly, they were not very friendly to us.[15]

It has already been noted that the Committee of Union and Progress grew and spread in Macedonia under the very noses of the European officers stationed there by the terms of the Mürzsteg agreement.[16] To what has already been said on that subject one might add the testimony of the well-known Austrian historian Heinrich Friedjung: "Even the German generals and instruction officers did not know what was being prepared in the officer-corps educated by them."[17] And General von der Goltz, who spent so many years training the Turkish army,

[12] D. S. Margoliouth, "Constantinople at the Declaration of the Constitution," *Fortnightly Review*, XC (October 1908), p. 563.

[13] *British Documents on the Origins of the War, 1898-1914*, vol. V, p. 263.

[14] *supra*, Chapter IV, note 61.

[15] Personal letter to the author, dated 16 May, 1941. In discussing his duties, Riza Tevfik is, of course, referring to the period after the proclamation of the constitution.

[16] *supra*, Chapter IV.

[17] *Das Zeitalter des Imperialismus 1884-1914* (Berlin, 1922), vol. II, p. 216.

wrote shortly after the Revolution: "Our diplomats have un-
justly been reproached for not foreseeing the occurrence of the
24th of July. Even many of those who took part directly were
most certainly surprised by it."[18]

The Young Turk Revolution, then, was a purely Turkish
enterprise—a nationalist uprising which aimed at the overthrowing of the régime of Abdul Hamid and its replacement by
a stronger government which would put an end to foreign
interference and to the intolerable conditions under which the
Turks had been living since the accession of Abdul Hamid. The
movement was liberal up to a point; that is to say a rudimentary
and ill-digested liberalism acquired from western Europe was
responsible to a large extent for the development of Turkish
nationalism; but as is almost always the case, the nationalistic
elements far outweighed the liberal. Very little thought was
given to the non-Turkish elements in the Ottoman Empire by
the victorious Young Turks other than that they must perforce
all become Ottomans in a revived and powerful empire capable
of holding up its head in the family of nations. The "Liberal"
party which formed the opposition in the years following the
Revolution was made up largely of those who inclined to the
views of Sabaheddin before the Revolution, but they never
really had a chance.

Even so, the Young Turks might have had a chance to work
out a better destiny for Turkey had they not almost at once felt
the pressure of European imperialism. The Revolution was no
sooner over than the Austrians despoiled them of the provinces
of Bosnia and Herzegovina, which, although they had really
been lost to the Turks since 1878, the Young Turks hoped to
recover. England, whose position immediately after the Revolution was paramount, mismanaged affairs so badly that she soon
turned the Young Turks against her once more. Italy despoiled
the empire of still more of its possessions, and finally it came

---

[18] C. Freiherr v. d. Goltz, "Die Innerpolitische Umwälzung in der Türkei,"
Deutsche Rundschau, XXXV (January 1909), p. 10.

to appear to the Young Turks that they had no friend but Germany once more.

On the other hand, it may be that the Young Turks had no possibility of success from the outset. They were inexperienced, and they possessed an empire which, like that of the Hapsburgs, was seething with incipient nationalism. That they made mistakes was only natural. Perhaps their greatest mistake was in keeping the Committee of Union and Progress as a faintly sinister and shadowy behind-the-scenes government instead of emerging once and for all and giving parliamentary government a fair trial. But they were kept from doing so by the same feeling of insecurity which caused them to leave Abdul Hamid on the throne.

In the last analysis, however, it seems likely that the Turks could never have solved the Eastern Question, the question which had been a shadow over Europe for two centuries and more, by themselves. Only by cutting adrift the non-Turkish areas and establishing a Turkish rather than an Ottoman nation could they hope for success, for the current of the times was setting against the multinational state.

BIBLIOGRAPHY

Bibliographical Notes

IN PREPARING THIS STUDY on the origins of the Young Turk movement it has been necessary to sift through an enormous amount of material of every conceivable type and value. The Committee of Union and Progress was a secret society, and it has understandably left behind no convenient record of its composition, organization, program, and activities. Thus it has been necessary to construct a connected picture of the Revolution which overthrew the system of Abdul Hamid, to piece it together from memoirs, from biographies, from secondary works of every description, and, not least of all, from newspaper and periodical accounts published at the time of the Young Turk Revolution and shortly thereafter.

In addition to the materials mentioned above, the author was fortunate enough to secure a number of letters from Turks who participated in the Revolution of 1908, some account of which would appear to be necessary.

During the academic year 1940-1941 I carried on a correspondence with my good friend, the late Dr. John Kingsley Birge, head of the Publication Department of the American Board of Foreign Missions in Istanbul. At his suggestion I prepared a brief list of questions concerning the Young Turk movement and sent them to him. Dr. Birge showed them to the late Jami Baykurt, former Turkish Minister of the Interior, who at once became interested in the matter. At his suggestion the questions were put into Turkish and circulated among a number of his acquaintances who, as young men, had taken part in the Revolution, with the request that they supply answers for the benefit of an "American professor" who was making a study of the Young Turk Revolution.

The responses were prompt and enthusiastic. Most of the replies were far more than brief answers to the questions asked, and from these letters it has been possible to fill in a number of gaps in information acquired elsewhere as well as to check material from other sources.

These letters are from men whose experiences were by no means identical. Fazlı Tung, for example, was among the young officers exiled in 1897 at the time of the defection of Murat Bey; Rahmi Bey was one of the founders of the new Committee of Union and Progress in Salonika; Ömer Fevzi Mardin was commander of the gendarmerie post at Gevgeli in Macedonia in 1908. Thus each is able to report on his own experiences in addition to discussing the general questions asked of him.

Dr. Ibrahim Temo answered Jami Bey's request for information with a copy of his recently published memoirs. (See below.) Jami Bey himself was kind enough to provide me with a manuscript copy of a chapter from his unpublished memoirs.

The two letters from the eminent Turkish philosopher and poet, the late Dr. Riza Tevfik, which are listed in the bibliography, were obtained through correspondence with that gentleman initiated at the suggestion of his daughter, Miss Selma Riza of New York. I was later fortunate enough to have several conversations with Riza Tevfik in Turkey.

The letter from Dr. Ernst Jäckh was in response to a letter from the author. Both letters simply put into writing the main points covered in a conversation we had in New York early in 1941.

The official publications of the European governments on the origins of the World War have been useful for the purposes of this study chiefly in a negative way. Only those to which reference has been made in the body of this work have been listed in the bibliography. In the main these publications demonstrate only that the Young Turk Revolution came as a surprise to the governments of Europe. They are useful in a secondary fashion, however, for the reports of diplomatic and consular officials immediately after the Revolution were quite full and the pictures they give of individuals and events most useful. On the whole, however, their value is neither more nor less than the value of reports after the fact made by other observers.

The materials listed under the heading of "Memoirs, Auto-biographies, etc.," are, as would be expected, by no means of equal value. From each something has been gained, but in many cases it has been very little indeed.

The memoirs of Dr. Ibrahim Temo, one of the founders of the first Committee of Union and Progress at the Military Medical School, must be counted as source material of the first order, particularly for the 1890's. Dr. Temo put together his memoirs long after the events and sometimes is not entirely clear, but the book is particularly valuable for the letters it reproduces.

Charles Roden Buxton's *Turkey in Revolution* appeared too early to be more than a recital of the events attendant upon the declaration of the Constitution in 1908. Buxton was a member of the Balkan Committee, and did, during the course of an official visit to Turkey after the Revolution, glean a few facts about the background of the movement, but, as he himself points out, the Committee of Union and Progress was still guarding its secrets well at this time.

Martin Hartmann's *Unpolitische Briefe aus der Türkei* is the work of a distinguished German Orientalist who also visited Turkey after the Revolution and set down his impressions and his interviews with various people. The work is one which must be quarried for odds and ends of information, but it definitely repays study. A useful index facilitates this quarrying, fortunately.

Gustav Hubka's *Die Osterreichisch-Ungarische Offiziers Mission in Makedonia 1903-1909* is interesting, like the official publications mentioned above, chiefly in a negative fashion, for it demonstrates that the Austrians as well were caught unprepared by the outbreak of the Revolution. However, Hubka's book presents many interesting sidelights on the relations between Turkish and foreign officers on the eve of the Revolution.

The only other item in the memoir category which needs to be singled out is *The Memoirs of Ismail Kemal Bey*, but sufficient attention has already been paid this work in the body of this study (cf. Chapter III). Its main interest is to be found in its description of the abortive plot to overthrow Abdul Hamid in 1903.

The biographies can be dismissed quickly. An even relatively adequate appraisal of Abdul Hamid has yet to be written in any language. The latest biography of the "Red Sultan," Alma Wittlin's *Abdul Hamid, the Shadow of God,* is nothing more than an attempt to psychoanalyze the man through a study of the meager literature available. As far as Atatürk is concerned, several fair to middling biographies have been written, but none of them is of any real value for the period before the World War.

Under "General Works" have been listed well over a hundred titles. Again it is obvious that not all are of great or even of much value.

Perhaps it would be well to preface the remarks on this category by noting that nothing like a serious study of the origins of the Young Turk Revolution has ever appeared in any language. A number of books have been written whose titles would suggest that one could properly expect to find an authoritative account of the subject between their covers, but appearances are often deceptive. Victor Bérard's *La Révolution Turque* is a study in international relations; Youssouf Fehmi's *La Révolution Ottomane (1908-1910)* has nothing on the origins of the Revolution; Vladan Georgevitch's *Die Türkische Revolution und ihre Aussichten* is chiefly the "Aussichten" from the Serbian point of view; E. F. Knight's *Turkey: The Awakening of Turkey: The Turkish Revolution of 1908* is a slipshod journalistic account written too soon after the events it describes but useful for the same purposes that Buxton's *Turkey in Revolution* serves; Graf Adalbert Sternberg's *Die Türkische Revolution* is very properly described by Martin Hartmann as "Die prätensiöse Deklamation von Nichtigkeiten."[1]

In Turkish there is a spate of literature on the Young Turk

[1] "Die neuere Literatur zum türkischen Problem," *Zeitschrift für Politik,* III (1909), 175.

Revolution, but much of it is of little value, and there is no single definitive study of the subject. The most useful works available are those of Ahmed Bedevi Kuran, but they are compendia of source material with connecting text rather than analytical studies.

Two other works dealing directly with the Young Turk Revolution I have not seen. One of these, A. Kutschbach's *Die Tuerkische Revolution*, is probably in a class with Steinberg's book if Kutschbach's memoirs are a fair sample of his writings. Of the other, Kh. Z. Gabidullin, *Mladoturetskaia Revolutsiia*, I know nothing.

Probably the most important single work in this category is Paul Fesch's *Constantinople aux Derniers Jours d'Abdul-Hamid*. This book was published in Paris in 1907, but the prophetic title does not imply that the author had advance knowledge of the Revolution of 1908. The belief was common at this time that Abdul Hamid was a dying man, and it was under this mistaken apprehension that Fesch gave his book the title it bears. Frequent reference to this book has been made in this study, for it contains a great amount of material on the Young Turks of Paris and the struggle for leadership between Ahmet Riza and Sabaheddin. Fesch, a French priest, interested himself in Sabaheddin, and his work displays a definite partisanship towards Sabaheddin, but his sympathies are fortunately represented in emphasis and interpretation rather than in distortion.

It has been suggested by Martin Hartmann that the real author of this book was Sabaheddin.[2] The fact that the book does contain much material of a documentary nature plus the fact that it does display such strong sympathy for Sabaheddin lends some credence to this thesis, but, on the other hand, the book contains much that has little to do with the Young Turk movement. The truth of the matter appears to be that Fesch wrote the chapter "La Jeune Turquie" from notes supplied by Fazlı Tung (Ahmet Fazlı Bey), who was Sabaheddin's foster-

---

[2] Cf. *Unpolitische Briefe aus der Türkei*, p. 41, where Hartmann refers to "[das grosse Werk] Sabaheddins, das er durch . . . Fesch veröffentlichen liess."

brother and who had recently escaped from Tripoli. So, at least, I was informed by the late Fazlı Tung through Jami Baykurt.

Another work which incorporates much material of a documentary nature is Joseph Denais' *La Turquie Nouvelle et l'Ancien Régime*. Denais was Fesch's secretary, but he does not seem to have possessed Fesch's fair-mindedness and moderation, for his book is a worshipful eulogy of Sabaheddin and a bitter denunciation of the latter's opponents. One feels that Denais was overawed by his association with "royalty" in the person of Sabaheddin. Nevertheless, the book is useful, although it duplicates in part some of the material in Fesch's work.

For the earliest period of the Young Turk movement a very useful supplement to the memoirs of Dr. Temo and the collection of Turkish letters referred to above is K. Süssheim's article "'Abd Allāh Djewdet," in the *Encyclopedia of Islam, Supplement* (1938). Süssheim must have derived his material from personal sources, for much of the information in his article had not, to my knowledge, appeared in print elsewhere.

That the Young Turk Revolution was a phenomenon of some interest to the rest of the world is attested by the number of articles on the subject which appeared in European and American periodicals during the course of the next few years. Everyone, it seems, who had any acquaintance with Turkey—and a great many who did not—wanted to express his ideas in print. Much that was of little significance appeared in this flood of material, but a number of interesting and useful articles found their way into print.

The outstanding contribution of this nature was made by General Imhoff in his article "Die Entstehung und der Zweck des Comités für Einheit und Fortschritt," *Die Welt des Islams*, I (1913). General Imhoff earned the gratitude of historians by patiently setting down everything which came to his ears concerning the origins of the Committee of Union and Progress during his tour of duty in Turkey and by publishing his findings with no comment other than the expressed hope that they would be of value to the future historian of the movement. His article is, then, in a class by itself, for it is a painstaking, impartial report of what Imhoff was told by Turkish officers and others who were in a position to know the facts when the subject was still fresh in their minds. When Imhoff gathered conflicting versions of the same story, he set them all down without attempting to decide which was the correct version.[8]

Of a documentary nature also are the articles by Afet and by Hüsrev Sami Kızıldoğan which appeared in 1937 in *Belleten*, the publication of the Turkish Historical Society which was founded in that year. Inasmuch as a discussion of these articles and those by Jean Deny in *Revue du Monde Musulmane* and *Revue des Études Islamiques* is to be found in the notes to Chapter IV above, no further comment will be made here.

Very useful studies of the Turkish army and the Revolution are provided in Felice de Chaurand de St-Eustache, "L'Esercito nel Movimento Costituzionale della Turchia," *Rivista d'Italia*, XI (1908); E. J. Dillon, "A Clue to the Turkish Tangle," *Contemporary Review*, XCV (1909); and Lieutenant-Colonel Malleterre, "L'Armée Jeune-Turque," *Revue des Sciences Politiques*, XXVI (1911).

Mention might also be made of the following articles which have been of some value: Richard Gottheil, "The Young Turks and Old Turkey," *Forum*, XL (1908); Gustav Hubka, "Die Reformaktion in Makedonien in den Jahren 1320-1324 (1904-1908)," *Streffleurs Militärische Zeitschrift* (1909), which supplements his book mentioned above (*Die Österreichisch-Ungarische Offiziersmission in Makedonia*); "Viator," "The Turkish Revolution," *Fortnightly Review*, XC (1908); and, despite their extreme bias, the articles on Sabaheddin published in *Asia* in 1924 by Demetra Vaka.

[8] Dr. Ernst Jäckh wrote to me on February 5, 1941, "General Imhoff war ein persönlicher Freund von mir, von dem ich nur sagen kann, dass er sich sehr genau informieren konnte und sehr sorgfältig zu berichten pflegte. Er ist eine zuverlässige Quelle."

Bibliography

OFFICIAL PUBLICATIONS

Germany. Auswärtiges Amt. *Die Grosse Politik der Europäischen Kabinette, 1871-1914. Sammlung der Diplomatischen Akten des Auswärtigen Amtes* (Berlin, 1922-1926). 40 vols.

Great Britain. *Accounts and Papers.* vol. cv (1909). Cmd. 4529. *Turkey. No. 1 (1909). Correspondence Respecting the Constitutional Movement in Turkey, 1908.*

Great Britain. Foreign Office. *British Documents on the Origins of the War, 1898-1914* (London, 1926ff.) 12 vols.

Soviet Russia. Tsentrarkhiv. A. Popov, "Turetskaia Revolutsiia 1908-1909 gg.," *Krasnyi Arkhiv,* XLIII (1930), 3-54; XLIV (1931), 3-39; XLV (1931), 27-52.

UNPUBLISHED MATERIALS

Baykurt, Jami (Cami Bey). Chapter from unpublished memoirs (in Turkish).

Jäckh, Dr. Ernst. Letter to the author dated February 5, 1941 (in German).

Janer (Caner), Fehmi. Letter to Jami Baykurt dated March 25, 1941 (in Turkish).

Kervan, Nahit. Letter to Jami Baykurt, undated (in Turkish).

Mardin, Ömer Fevzi. Letter to Jami Baykurt dated March 4, 1941 (in Turkish).

Onbulak, Dr. Ali Osman. Letter to Jami Baykurt dated March 20, 1941 (in Turkish).

Özden, Dr. Akil Muhtar. Letter to Jami Baykurt dated May 4, 1941 (in Turkish).

Rahmi Bey. Letter to Jami Baykurt dated March 9, 1941 (in Turkish).

Riza Tevfik Bey. Letter to the author dated May 16, 1941 (in English).

—— Letter to the author dated May 24, 1942 (in English).

Tung, Fazlı. Letter to Jami Baykurt dated May 20, 1941 (in Turkish).

MEMOIRS, AUTOBIOGRAPHIES, DIARIES, PERSONAL NARRATIVES, ETC.

Abbott, G. F. *The Tale of a Tour in Macedonia* (London: Edward Arnold, 1903). 343 pp.

Aflalo, F. G. *Regilding the Crescent* (London: Martin Secker, 1911). 310 pp.

Bolayır, Enver (ed.). *Talât Paşa'nın Hatıraları* [*Memoirs of Talat Pasha*] (Istanbul: Güven Basımevi, 1946). 149 pp.

Bonsal, Stephen. *Heyday in a Vanished World* (New York: W. W. Norton, 1937). 445 pp.

Buxton, Charles Roden. *Turkey in Revolution* (London: T. Fisher Unwin, 1909). 285 pp.

Dukagjin-Zadeh Basri-Bey. *Le Monde Oriental et l'avenir de la Paix* (4th edn.; Paris: Perrin, 1920). 320 pp.

Edib, Halidé. *Memoirs of Halidé Edib* (New York & London: Century, n.d.). 472 pp.

Farkas, Paul. *Staatsstreich und Gegenrevolution in der Türkei* (Berlin: Puttkammer & Mühlbrecht, 1909). 110 pp.

Fraser, David. *Persia and Turkey in Revolt* (Edinburgh & London: William Blackwood & Sons, 1910). 440 pp.

Fidel, Camille. *Les Premiers Jours de la Turquie Libre: Lettres d'un Témoin* (Paris: Société Général d'Imprimerie, 1909). 77 pp.

Giesl, Wladimir. *Zwei Jahrzehnte im Nahen Orient: Aufzeichnungen des Generals der Kavallerie Baron Wladimir Giesl*. Ed. by General-major Ritter v. Steinitz. (Berlin: Verlag für Kulturpolitik, 1927). 331 pp.

Giolitti, Giovanni. *Memoirs of My Life* (London & Sydney: Chapman & Dodd, 1923). 472 pp.

Hartmann, Martin. *Unpolitische Briefe aus der Türkei*. vol. III of *Der Islamische Orient: Berichte und Forschungen* (Leipzig: Rudolf Haupt, 1910). 262 pp.

Hepworth, Geo. H. *Through Armenia on Horseback* (New York: E. P. Dutton, 1898). 355 pp.

Herbert, Aubrey. *Ben Kendim: A Record of Eastern Travel* (2nd edn.; London: Hutchinson, n.d.). 380 pp.

Hubka, Gustav. *Die Österreichisch-Ungarische Offiziersmission in Makedonia 1903-1909*. Im Auftrage des letzten K. u. K. Militäradjoints, Oberst im Generalstabkorps August Urbánski von Ostrymiecz und mit Genehmigung des K. u. K. Reichskriegsministerium bearbeitet von Gustav Hubka (Vienna: F. Tempsky, 1910). 154 pp.

Ismail Kemal Bey. *The Memoirs of Ismail Kemal Bey*. Ed. by Sommerville Story (London: Constable, 1920). 410 pp.

Izzet Pascha. *Denkwürdigkeiten des Marschalls Izzet Pascha; ein kritischer Beitrag zur Kriegsschuldfrage*. Ed. & tr. by Karl Klinghardt (Leipzig: K. F. Koehler, 1927). 309 pp.

Jäckh, Ernst. *Der Aufsteigende Halbmond: Beiträge zur Türkischen Renaissance* (Berlin: Buchverlag der "Hilfe," 1911). 197 pp.

———— (ed.) *Kiderlen-Wächter, der Staatsmann und Mensch: Briefwechsel und Nachlass* (Berlin & Leipzig: Deutsche Verlags-Anstalt Stuttgart, 1925). 2 vols.

———— *The Rising Crescent; Turkey Yesterday, Today, and Tomorrow* (New York & Toronto: Farrar & Rinehart, 1944). 278 pp.

Kutschbach, A. *Der Brandherd Europas: 50 Jahre Balkan-Erinnerungen* (Leipzig: E. Haberland, 1929). 455 pp.

Mayakon, İsmail Müştak. *Yıldızda Neler Gördüm? [What did I See at Yıldız?]*. (Istanbul: Sertel Matbaası, 1940). 200 pp.

BIBLIOGRAPHY

Midhat, Ali Haydar. *Souvenir de mon Exil Volontaire* (Geneva: Imprimerie Internationale, 1905). 222 pp. plus 34 pp. in Turkish.
Mithat, Ali Haydar. *Hatıralarım, 1872-1946 [My Memories, 1872-1946]*. (Istanbul: Mithat Akçıt Yayını, 1946). 366 pp.
Moore, Arthur. *The Orient Express* (London: Constable, 1914). 308 pp.
Niyazi, Kolağası [Major] Resnalı Ahmet. *Hatıratı Niyazi, yahut Tarihçe-i-İnkılâb-ı-Kebir-i-Osmaniden bir Sahife [The Memoirs of Niyazi, or a Page from the History of the Great Ottoman Revolution]*. (Istanbul: Sabah Matbaası, 1326 [1908/1909]). 240 pp.
Patrick, Mary Mills. *Under Five Sultans* (New York & London: Century, 1929). 357 pp.
Pears, Sir Edwin. *Forty Years in Constantinople* (New York: Appleton, 1916). 390 pp.
Pomiankowski, Joseph. *Der Zusammenbruch des Ottomanischen Reiches: Erinnerungen an die Türkei aus der Zeit des Weltkrieges* (Zurich, Leipzig, Vienna: Amalthea Verlag, 1928). 444 pp.
Poynter, Mary A. *When Turkey was Turkey: In and Around Constantinople* (London: Routledge; New York: Dutton, 1921). 197 pp.
Rambert, Louis. *Notes et Impressions de Turquie: L'Empire Ottoman sous Abdul-Hamid 1895-1905* (Geneva & Paris: Edition Atar, 1926). 355 pp.
Rappoport, Alfred. *Au Pays des Martyrs: Notes et Souvenirs d'un ancien Consul-Général d'Autriche-Hongrie en Macédoine (1904-1909)* (Paris: J. Gamber, 1927). 137 pp.
Sciaky, Leon. *Farewell to Salonica: Portrait of an Era* (New York: Current Books; A. A. Wyn, 1946). 241 pp.
Steed, Henry Wickham. *Through Thirty Years 1892-1922; A Personal Narrative* (Garden City, N.Y.: Doubleday Page, 1925). 2 vols.
Stuermer, Dr. Harry. *Two War Years in Constantinople: Sketches of German and Young Turkish Ethics and Politics* (New York: G. H. Doran, 1917). 292 pp.
Tahsin Paşa. *Abdülhamit ve Yıldız Hatıraları [Abdul Hamid and Memories of Yildiz]* (Istanbul: Ahmet Halit Kitaphanesi, 1931). 297 pp.
Temo, Dr. Ibrahim. *İttihad ve Terakki Cemiyetinin Tesekkülü ve Hidematı Vataniye ve İnkılâbı Milliye Dair Hatıratım* (The Formation of the Society of Union and Progress and my Memories respecting Services to the Fatherland and the National Revolution) (Medjidia, Romania, n.p., 1939). 303 pp.
Upward, Allen. *The East End of Europe: The Report of an Unofficial Mission to the European Provinces of Turkey on the Eve of the Revolution* (London: John Murray, 1908). 368 pp.
Vambéry, Arminius. *The Story of My Struggles: The Memoirs of Arminius Vambéry* (New York: E. P. Dutton, 1904). 2 vols.
Whitman, Sidney. *Turkish Memories* (London: Wm. Heinemann, 1914). 305 pp.
Woods, Sir Henry F. *Spunyarn from the Strands of a Sailor's Life Afloat*

and Ashore: Forty-seven Years under the Ensigns of Great Britain and Turkey (London: Hutchinson, 1924). 2 vols.

BIOGRAPHIES

Armstrong, H. C. *Grey Wolf: Mustafa Kemal, an Intimate Study of a Dictator* (London: Arthur Barker, 1932). 352 pp.

Deny, Jean (ed.). *Souvenirs du Gâzi Moustafa Kemâl Pacha* (Paris: Librarie Orientaliste Paul Geuthner, 1927). pp. 117-221; 459-463. Extracted from the *Révue des Études Islamiques* (1927).

Djemaleddin Bey. *Sultan Murad V: The Turkish Dynastic Mystery 1876-1895* (London: Kegan Paul, Trench, Trübner, 1895). 266 pp.

Dorys (Adossidès), Georges. *The Private Life of the Sultan of Turkey* (New York: D. Appleton, 1902). 277 pp.

Elmalch, Abraham. *Le Professeur Abraham Galante: Sa Vie et ses Oeuvres* (Istanbul: n.p., 1946). 104 pp.

Froembgen, Hanns. *Kemal Ataturk: A Biography*. Tr. by Kenneth Kirkness (London: Jarrolds, 1937). 286 pp.

Gentizon, Paul. *Mustapha Kemal ou l'Orient en Marche* (Paris: Bossard, 1929). 350 pp.

Heyd, Uriel. *Foundations of Turkish Nationalism: The Life and Teachings of Ziya Gökalp* (London: Luzac & Co., & the Harvill Press, 1950). 174 pp.

Hidayette. *Abdul Hamid Révolutionnaire, ou ce qu'on ne peu pas dire en Turquie* (n.p., n.d.). 269 pp.

Ikbal Ali Shah. *Kamal: Maker of Modern Turkey* (London: Herbert Joseph, 1934). 297 pp.

Léouzon le Duc, L. *Midhat Pacha* (Paris: E. Dentin, 1877). 227 pp.

Lusignan, Princess Annie de. *The Twelve Years' Reign of his Imperial Majesty Abdul Hamid II, Sultan of Turkey* (London: Sampson Low, Marston, Searle, & Rivington, 1889). 270 pp.

Midhat, Ali Haydar. *The Life of Midhat Pasha; a Record of his Services, Political Reforms, Banishment, and Judicial Murder* (London: John Murray, 1903). 292 pp.

Mikusch, Dagobert von. *Mustapha Kemal: Between Europe and Asia; a Biography*. Tr. by John Linton (Garden City, N.Y.: Doubleday, Doran, 1931). 380 pp.

Nüzhet, Sadettin. *Namık Kemal: Hayatı ve Şiirleri* (Istanbul: Yeni Şark Kitaphanesi, 1933). 139 plus 251 pp.

Pakalın, Mehmed Zeki. *Midhat Paşa* (Istanbul: Ahmet Sait Matbaası, 1940). 259 pp.

Pears, Sir Edwin. *Life of Abdul Hamid* (New York: Henry Holt, 1917). 365 pp.

Rizas, G. *Abdul Hamid: Sa Vie Politique et Intime; 33 Ans de Tyrannie; Tous les Secrets de la Camarilla dévoilés; Prodigeux Efforts du Parti Jeune Turc; publié par G. Rizas d'après les Meilleurs Écrivains et Biographes d'Abdul Hamid* (Constantinople: Imprimerie E. Pallamary, 1909). 496 pp.

Roy, Gilles. *Abdul-Hamid, le Sultan Rouge* (Paris: Payot, 1936). 243 pp.
Şapolyo, Enver Behnan. *Ziya Gökalp: İttihat ve Terakki ve Meşrutiyet Tarihi* [*Ziya Gökalp: History of Union and Progress and the Constitution*] (Istanbul: Güven Basımevi, 1943). 270 pp.
Tongas, Gérard. *Atatürk and the True Nature of Modern Turkey*. Tr. by Major F. F. Rynd (London: Luzac, 1939). 79 pp.
Wittlin, Alma. *Abdul Hamid, the Shadow of God*. Tr. from the German by Norman Denny (London: John Lane, 1940). 296 pp.
Wortham, H. E. *Mustapha Kemal of Turkey* (Boston: Little, Brown, 1931). 251 pp.

GENERAL WORKS

Abbott, G. F *Turkey in Transition* (London: Edward Arnold, 1909). 370 pp.
Abelous, Frédéric. *L'Évolution de la Turquie dans ses Rapports avec les Étrangers* (Toulouse: Imprimerie du Sud-Quest, 1928). 297 pp.
Ahmet Riza. *La Crise de l'Orient* (Paris, 1907).
——— *La Faillite Morale de la Politique Occidentale en Orient* (Paris: Picart, 1922). 207 pp.
——— *Tolérance Musulmane* (Paris, 1897).
Aischin, Mohamed. *Die Freiheitsbewegung in der Türkei* (*Ein Versuch historischer Forschung*). Einzig autorisierte Uebersetzung von A. J. Ramm (Berlin: J. Ladyschnikow, 1908). 91 pp.
Allen, Henry Elisha. *The Turkish Transformation: A Study in Social and Religious Development* (Chicago: University of Chicago Press, 1935). 251 pp.
Allen, W. E. D. *The Turks in Europe; a Sketch-Study* (New York: Scribner's 1920). 256 pp.
Anastasoff, Christ. *The Tragic Peninsula: A History of the Macedonian Movement for Independence since 1878* (St. Louis, Mo.: Blackwell Wielandy Co., 1938). 369 pp.
Ancel, Jacques. *Manuel Historique de la Question d'Orient* (*1792-1926*) (3rd ed.; Paris: Librairie Delagrave, 1927). 340 pp.
Antonius, George. *The Arab Awakening: The Story of the Arab National Movement* (Philadelphia, New York, Toronto: Lippincott, 1939). 471 pp.
Babinger, Franz. *Die Geschichtsschreiber der Osmanen und ihre Werke* (Leipzig: Otto Harrassowitz, 1927). 477 pp.
Baker, B. Granville. *The Passing of the Turkish Empire in Europe* (London: Seeley, Service, & Co., 1913). 335 pp.
Bareilles, Bertrand. *Les Turcs; ce que fut leur Empire, leurs Comédies Politiques* (Paris: Perrin, 1917). 313 pp.
Becker, Carl Heinrich. *Islamstudien: Vom Werden und Wesen der Islamischen Welt* (Leipzig: Quelle & Meyer, 1932). 2 vols.
Bérard, Victor. *La Mort de Stamboul: Considérations sur le Gouvernement des Jeunes-Turcs* (Paris: Colin, 1913). 418 pp.

———— *La Révolution Turque* (Paris: Armand Colin, 1909). 352 pp.

Birge, John Kingsley. *The Bektashi Order of Dervishes* (London: Luzac; Hartford, Conn.: Hartford Seminary Press, 1937). 291 pp.

Blaisdell, Donald C. *European Financial Control in the Ottoman Empire: A Study of the Establishment, Activities, and Significance of the Administration of the Ottoman Public Debt* (New York: Columbia University Press, 1929). 243 pp.

Brockelmann, Carl. *Geschichte der Islamischen Völker und Staaten* (Munich & Berlin: R. Oldenbourg, 1939). 495 pp.

Brown, John P. *The Dervishes, or Oriental Spiritualism.* Ed. with introduction and notes by H. A. Rose (London: Humphrey Milford, 1927). 496 pp.

Carra de Vaux, Baron. *Les Penseurs de l'Islam* (Paris: Paul Geuthner, 1921-1926). 5 vols.

Castle, Wilfred T. F. *Grand Turk: An Historical Outline of Life and Events, of Culture and Politics, of Trade and Travel during the Last Years of the Ottoman Empire and the First Years of the Turkish Republic* (London, New York, Melbourne: Hutchinson & Co., n.d. [1943?]). 170 pp.

The Cause of World Unrest, With an Introduction by the Editor of "The Morning Post" (London: Grant Richards Ltd., 1920). 269 pp.

Cohen, M[arcel Samuel Raphael] ("Tekin Alp"). *Türkismus und Pantürkismus.* Vol. 2 of Deutsche Orient-Bücherei, ed. by Ernst Jäckh (Weimar: Verlag Gustav Kiepenheuer, 1915). 112 pp.

Davey, Richard. *The Sultan and his Subjects* (New York: E. P. Dutton, 1897). 2 vols.

David, Wade Dewood. *European Diplomacy in the Near Eastern Question, 1906-1909*, Illinois Studies in the Social Sciences, vol. xxv, No. 4 (Urbana, Ill.: University of Illinois Press, 1940). 124 pp.

Denais, Joseph. *La Turquie Nouvelle et l'Ancien Régime* (Paris: Librairie des Sciences Politiques et Sociales; Marcel Rivière, 1909). 96 pp.

Diamantopulo, Hercule. *Le Réveil de la Turquie: Études et Croquis Historiques* (Alexandria, Egypt: I. Della Rocca, n.d. [1909?]). 300 pp.

Dubnow, S. M. *Die Neueste Geschichte des Jüdischen Volkes* (Berlin: Jüdischer Verlag, 1920-1923). 3 vols.

Durand, Alfred. *Jeune Turquie Vieille France* (Paris: Fournier, 1909). 355 pp.

Edib, Halidé. *Turkey Faces West: A Turkish View of Recent Changes and their Origin* (New Haven: Yale University Press, 1930). 273 pp.

Eliot, Sir Charles ("Odysseus"). *Turkey in Europe* (New edn.; London: Edward Arnold, 1908). 459 pp.

Emin, Ahmed. *The Development of Modern Turkey as Measured by its Press*, Studies in History, Economics and Public Law edited by the Faculty of Political Science of Columbia University, vol. LIX, No. 1 (New York: Columbia University, 1914). 143 pp.

163

Emin, Ahmed. *Die Türkei*, Vol. 5 of Perthes' Kleine Völker- und Länder-kunde zum Gebrauch im praktischen Leben (Gotha: Perthes, 1918). 95 pp.

Endres, Franz Carl. *Die Türkei: Eine Einführung in das Verständnis von Land und Volk* (4th ed.; Munich: Oskar Beck, 1918). 325 pp.

Fazy, Edmond. *Les Turcs d'aujourd'hui ou le grand Karaghuez* (Paris: Paul Ollendorf, 1898). 284 pp.

Fehmi, Youssouf. *La Révolution Ottomane (1908-1910)* (Paris: V. Giard & E. Brière, 1911). 282 pp.

———— *Tablettes Révolutionnaires d'un Jeune Turc* (Paris: A. Michalon, 1903). 69 pp.

———— *Les Turcs de Paris: Espionnage et Contre-Police* (Paris: André Lequesne, 1908). 46 pp.

Fesch, Paul. *Constantinople aux Derniers Jours d'Abdul-Hamid* (Paris: Marcel Rivière, 1907). 673 pp.

Friedjung, Heinrich. *Das Zeitalter des Imperialismus 1884-1914* (Berlin: Neufeld & Henius, 1922). 2 vols.

Fua, Albert. *Abdul-Hamid II et Mourad V: Masque de Fer* (Paris: A. Michalon, 1909). 76 pp.

———— *Le Comité Union et Progrès Contre la Constitution* (Paris: Emile Nourry, n.d. [1912?]). 107 pp.

Fua, Albert, and Refik-Nevzad, Dr. *La Trahison du Gouvernement Turc (Comité Union et Progrès)* (Paris: Michel, 1914). 31 pp.

Gabidullin, Kh. Z. *Mladoturetskaia Revolutsiia* (Moscow: Istoricheskie Ocherki, 1936). 227 pp.

Galanté, Abraham. *Nouveaux Documents sur Sabbetai Sevi: Organisation et Us et Coutumes de ses Adeptes* (Istanbul: Fratelli Haim, 1935). 125 pp.

———— *Turcs et Juifs: Étude Historique, Politique* (Istanbul: Haim, Rozio & Co., 1932). 160 pp.

———— *Appendice à l'ouvrage Turcs et Juifs* (Istanbul: M. Babok, 1937). 40 pp.

Garcia, Louis. *The Great Powers and the Macedonian Question, 1902-1908* (unpublished M.A. thesis, University of California, 1934). 117 numbered leaves.

Georgevitch, T.-R. *La Macédoine* (Paris: Grasset, 1919). 273 pp.

Georgevitch, Vladan. *Die Türkische Revolution und ihre Aussichten* (Leipzig: S. Hirzel, 1908). 102 pp.

Georgiades, Demetrius. *Is the Regeneration of Turkey Possible?* (London: Kegan Paul, Trench, Trübner, 1910). 163 pp.

Ghersi, Emanuele. *I Movimenti Nazionalistici nel Mondo Musulmano* (Padova: Cedam, 1932). 336 pp.

Gibb, E. J. W. *A History of Ottoman Poetry* (London: Luzac, 1900-1909). 6 vols.

des Godins de Souhesmes, G. *Au Pays des Osmanlis* (2nd edn.; Paris: Victor-Havard, 1894). 400 pp.

Goltz, Freiherr von der. *Der Jungen Türkei Niederlage und die Möglich-keit ihrer Wiedererhebung* (Berlin: Verlag von Gebrüder Paetel, 1913). 70 pp.

Graves, Philip P. *Briton and Turk* (London & Melbourne: Hutchinson, 1941). 260 pp.

Hamilton, Angus. *Problems of the Middle East* (London: Evleigh Nash, 1909). 484 pp.

Hasluck, F. W. *Christianity and Islam under the Sultans.* Ed. by Margaret M. Hasluck (Oxford: Clarendon Press, 1929). 2 vols.

Hecquard, Charles. *La Turquie sous Abdul-Hamid II: Exposé Fidèle de la Gérance d'un Empire pendant un quart de Siècle (31 Août 1876-1er Septembre 1900)* (Brussels: Henri Lamertin, 1901). 468 pp.

Helfferich, Karl. *Die Deutsche Türkenpolitik* (Berlin: Vossische Verlag, 1921). 31 pp.

Imbert, Paul. *La Renovation de l'Empire Ottoman: Affaires de Turquie* (Paris: Perrin, 1909). 311 pp.

Jarman, T. L. *Turkey* (Bristol: Arrowsmith, 1935). 132 pp.

Jung, Eugene. *La Revolte Arabe* (Paris: C. Bohrer, 1924-1925). 2 vols.

Knight, E. F. *Turkey: The Awakening of Turkey: The Turkish Revolu-tion of 1908* (Boston & Tokyo: J. B. Millet Co., 1910). 324 pp.

Kohn, Hans. *A History of Nationalism in the East* (New York: Harcourt, Brace, 1929). 476 pp.

Kuran, Ahmed Bedevi. *İnkılâp Tarihimiz ve İttihad ve Terakki* [*The His-tory of our Revolution and Union and Progress*] (Istanbul: Tan Matbaası, 1948). 319 pp.

——— *İnkılâp Tarihimiz ve "Jön Turkler"* [*The History of Our Revolution and the "Young Turks"*] (Istanbul: Tan Matbaası, 1945). 378 pp.

Kutschbach, A. *Die Tuerkische Revolution* (Halle, 1908).

La Jonquiere, Vicomte de. *Histoire de l'Empire Ottoman depuis les Origines jusqu'a nos jours* (Nouvelle ed.; Paris: Librairie Hachette, 1914). 2 vols.

Lamouche, Colonel, *Histoire de la Turquie depuis les Origines jusqu'a nos jours* (Paris: Payot, 1934). 427 pp.

——— *Quinze Ans d'Histoire Balkanique (1904-1918)* (Paris: Payot, 1928). 234 pp.

Langer, William L. *The Diplomacy of Imperialism 1890-1902* (New York: Alfred A. Knopf, 1935). 2 vols.

Lévy, Sam. *Le Déclin du Croissant* (Paris: Bernard Grasset, 1913). 231 pp.

Loutfi, I. *L'État Politique de la Turquie et le Parti Libéral* (Paris: Im-primerie d'Ouvriers Sourds-Muets, 1903). 32 pp.

Lukach, Harry Charles (Sir Harry Luke). *The City of Dancing Dervishes and other Sketches and Studies from the Near East* (London: Mac-millan, 1914). 257 pp.

Luke, Sir Harry. *The Making of Modern Turkey; from Byzantium to Angora* (London: Macmillan, 1936). 246 pp.

McCullagh, Francis. *The Fall of Abd-ul-Hamid* (London: Methuen, 1910). 316 pp.

Macdonald, John. *Turkey and the Eastern Question* (London: T. C. & E. C. Jack, 1913). 92 pp.

Mandelstam, André. *Le Sort de l'Empire Ottoman* (Lausanne & Paris: Payot, 1917). 631 pp.

Mantegazza, Vico. *La Turchia Liberale e le Questioni Balchaniche* (Milano: Fratelli Treves, 1908). 424 pp.

Mears, Eliot Grinnell. *Modern Turkey: A Politico-Economic Interpretation with selected chapters by Representative Authorities* (New York: Macmillan, 1924). 779 pp.

Midhat, Kemal. *La Turquie Nouvelle* (Geneva: Edition Atar, n.d.). 16 pp.

Miller, William. *The Ottoman Empire and its Successors, 1801-1927, with an Appendix, 1927-1936* (Rev. and enlarged ed.; Cambridge: At the University Press, 1936). 644 pp.

Moulin, René. *Force et Faiblesse de la Jeune-Turquie* (Paris: Plon-Nourrit, 1910). 87 pp.

Mourad-bey (Murat Bey). *La Force et la Faiblesse de la Turquie: Les Coupables et les Innocents* (Geneva: J. Mouille, 1897). 59 pp.

———— *Le Palais de Yildiz et la Sublime Porte: Le Véritable Mal d'Orient* (Paris: Chaix, 1895). 47 pp.

Muhiddin, Ahmet. *Die Kulturbewegung im Modernen Türkentum* (Leipzig: J. M. Gebhardt, 1921). 72 pp.

Nicolaïdès, N. *Sa Majesté Imperiale, Abd-Ul-Hamid Khan II, Sultan, Réformateur et Réorganisateur de l'Empire Ottoman* (Brussels: Th. Dewarichet, 1907). 110 pp.

———— *Une Année de Constitution: 11/24 Juillet 1908-11/24 Juillet 1909* (Brussels: Th. Dewarichet, 1909). 262 pp.

Nouri, Ali. *Unter dem Scepter des Sultans* (Berlin: E. A. Schwetschke, 1905). 216 pp.

Pinon, René. *L'Europe et l'Empire Ottoman* (Paris: Perrin, 1917). 603 pp.

———— *L'Europe et la Jeune Turquie* (Paris: Perrin, 1911). 500 pp.

Queenborough, Lady (Edith Star Miller). *Occult Theocrasy* (Privately printed: n.p., n.d.). 2 vols.

Risal, P. *La Ville Convoitée: Salonique* (Paris: Perrin, 1914). 368 pp.

Riza, Ahmet. See Ahmet Riza.

Rousseau, Louis. *L'Effort Ottoman* (Paris: F. R. de Rudeval, 1908). 355 pp.

Ruchti, Jacob. *Die Reformaktion Österreich-Ungarns und Russlands in Mazedonien 1903-1908; die Durchführung der Reformen* (Gotha: Perthes, 1918). 104 pp.

Salmoné, H. Anthony. *The Fall and the Resurrection of Turkey* (London: Methuen, 1896). 271 pp.

Sarrou, A. *La Jeune Turquie et la Révolution* (Paris: Berger-Levrault, 1912). 268 pp.

BIBLIOGRAPHY

Sax, Carl Ritter von. *Geschichte des Machtverfalls der Türkei bis Ende des 19. Jahrhunderts, und die Phasen der "Orientalischen Frage" bis auf die Gegenwart* (Vienna: Manz, 1913). 654 pp.

Seignobosc, II. *Turcs et Turquie* (Paris: Payot, 1920). 249 pp.

Seton-Watson, R. W. *The Rise of Nationality in the Balkans* (London: Constable, 1917). 308 pp.

Stern, Bernhard. *Abdul Hamid II: Seine Familie und sein Hofstaat: Nach eigenen Ermittelungen* (Budapest: Sigmund Deutsch, 1901). 234 pp.

—— *Jungtürken und Verschwörer: Die Innere Lage der Türkei unter Abdul Hamid II: Nach eigenen Ermittelungen und Mittheilungen Osmanischer Parteiführer* (2nd edn.; Leipzig: Grübel & Sommerlatte, 1901). 263 pp.

—— *Der Sultan und seine Politik: Erinnerungen und Beobachtungen eines Journalisten* (Leipzig: B. Elischer Nachfolger, 1906). 240 pp.

Sternberg, Graf Adalbert. *Die Türkische Revolution* (Berlin: Georg Stillke, 1909). 118 pp.

Süssheim, K. "'Abd Allāh Djewdet," *Encyclopedia of Islam, Supplement* (1938), pp. 55-60.

—— "Der Zusammenbruch des Türkischen Reiches in Europa," in *Die Balkanfrage*, Heft 3 of Veröffentlichungen der Handelshochschule (München & Leipzig: Dunker & Humblot, 1914), pp. 69-107.

Swire, J. *Bulgarian Conspiracy* (London: Robert Hale, 1939). 356 pp.

Sykes, Sir Mark. *The Caliph's Last Heritage: A Short History of the Turkish Empire* (London: Macmillan, 1915). 638 pp.

Toynbee, Arnold J., and Kirkwood, Kenneth P. *Turkey* (New York: Scribner's, 1927). 329 pp.

Ular, Alexander, and Insabato, Enrico. *Der Erlöschende Halbmond: Türkische Enthüllungen* (Frankfurt a.M.: Rütten & Loening, 1909). 343 pp.

Valyi, Felix. *Spiritual and Political Revolutions in Islam* (London: Kegan Paul, Trench, Trübner, 1925). 236 pp.

Vambéry, Hermann (Arminius). *Der Islam im Neunzehnten Jahrhundert: Eine Culturgeschichtliche Studie* (Leipzig: F. A. Brockhaus, 1875). 321 pp.

—— *Western Culture in Eastern Lands: A Comparison of the Methods Adopted by England and Russia in the Middle East* (New York: E. P. Dutton, 1906). 410 pp.

Vivian, Herbert. *Secret Societies Old and New* (London: T. Butterworth, 1927). 306 pp.

Waugh, Sir Telford. *Turkey Yesterday, Today, and Tomorrow* (London: Chapman & Hall, 1930). 305 pp.

Webster, Nesta H. *Secret Societies and Subversive Movements* (London: Boswell, 1928). 419 pp.

White, Wilbur W. *The Process of Change in the Ottoman Empire* (Chicago: University of Chicago Press, 1937). 315 pp.

Wichtl, Friederich. *Weltfreimauerei: Weltrevolution: Weltrepublik: Eine Untersuchung über Ursprung und Endziele des Weltkrieges* (5th edn.; Munich: J. F. Lehmanns Verlag, 1920). 280 pp.

Williams, Talcott. *Turkey, a World Problem of Today* (Garden City, N.Y.: Doubleday, Page, 1921). 336 pp.

Wilson, Samuel Graham. *Modern Movements among Moslems* (New York & London: Fleming H. Revell Co., 1916). 305 pp.

Young, George. *Constantinople* (London: Methuen; New York: G. H. Doran, n.d. [1925?]). 310 pp.

Zimmerer, Heinrich. "Die Europäische Türkei und Armenien," Part III of *Helmolt's Weltgeschichte*, vol. v, pp. 117-212 (Leipzig & Vienna: Bibliographisches Institut, 1905).

PERIODICAL MATERIAL

"Abdul Hamid, Sultan and Khalif, and the Pan-Islamic Movement," *Blackwood's Magazine*, CLXXX (Sept., 1906), 291-310.

"Abdul Hamid: The Man, his Character, and his Entourage," *Pall Mall Magazine*, XXX (May-Aug., 1903), 261-270.

Âfet. "Le Revolver Sacré," *Belleten*, 1 (July-Oct., 1937), 611-617.

—— "La Société 'Patrie et Liberté,' " *Belleten*, 1 (April, 1937), 299-309.

d'Agostino, Charles. "La Littérature turque contemporaine," *Revue Encyclopédique*, v (Sept., 1895), 345-350.

Ahmet Riza. "Le Calife et ses Devoirs," *Revue Occidentale*, 2nd series, XII (July, 1896), 93-98.

—— "Der Fatalismus," *Das Freie Wort*, VIII (Aug., 1908), 352-355.

—— "L'Inaction des Jeunes-Turcs," *Revue Occidentale*, 2nd series, XXVII (Jan., 1903), 91-98.

—— "Tolerance Musulmane," *Revue Occidentale*, 2nd series, XII (Nov., 1896), 304-317.

"The Armenians and the 'Young Turks,' " *Armenia*, III (May-June, 1907), 24-28.

Babin, Gustave. "La Révolution Turque," *L'Illustration*, LXVI (Aug., 1908), 141-144.

Bedikian, Dikran Mardiros. "The Silent Revolution in Turkey," *The World's Work*, XVI (Oct., 1908), 10825-10829.

Beesly, E. S. "The Turkish Revolution," *The Positivist Review*, XVI (Sept., 1908), 201-205.

Bilinski, Rustem Bey de. "The Situation in Turkey," *Fortnightly Review*, LXXVIII (Feb., 1902), 86-102.

—— "The Turkish Army," *Contemporary Review*, XCII (Sept., 1907), 403-409.

—— "The Turkish Revolution," *Nineteenth Century*, LXIV (Sept., 1908), 353-372.

Blind, Karl. "The Prorogued Turkish Parliament," *North American Review*, CLXXV (July, 1902), 42-52.

———— "Young Turkey," *Fortnightly Review*, LXVI (Dec., 1896), 830-843.

Bruno de Paris, Fr. "Choses d'Orient: La Révolution en Turquie," *Études Franciscaines*, XXI (Jan.-Feb., 1909), 5-20; 146-162.

Buxton, Noel. "The Young Turks," *Nineteenth Century*, LXV (Jan., 1909), 16-24.

C. E. B. "Notes sur le Panislamisme," *Questions Diplomatiques et Coloniales*, XXVIII (1909), 641-656; 729-742.

Charlton, Zeeneb. "Six Osmanli Patriots," *Nineteenth Century*, LXXIV (Dec., 1913), 1220-1229.

de Chaurand de St-Eustache, Felice. "L'Esercito nel Movimento Costituzionale della Turchia," *Rivista d'Italia*, XI (Oct., 1908), 513-532.

Choublier, Max. "Les Bektachis et la Roumélie," *Revue des Études Islamiques*, I (1927), 427-453.

"The Committee of Union and Progress," *The Spectator*, CI (Dec., 1908), 1087-1088.

"The Diary of a Turk," *Athenaeum*, I (193), 814-815.

Dillon, E. J. "A Clue to the Turkish Tangle," *Contemporary Review*, XCV (1909), 743-756.

———— "The Reforming Turk," *Quarterly Review*, CCX (Jan., 1909), 231-253.

———— "The Unforeseen Happens as Usual," *Contemporary Review*, XCIV (Sept., 1908), 364-384.

"The Doctrine of Ascendancy," *The Round Table*, V (1914-1915), 70-102.

Dorobantz, Jacques. "La Crise Turque," *Questions Diplomatiques et Coloniales*, XXVI (Aug., 1908), 205-214.

———— "Les Jeunes-Turcs et la Macédoine," *Questions Diplomatiques et Coloniales*, XXVI (Sept., 1908), 279-288.

Elliott, Sir Henry. "The Death of Abdul Aziz and of Turkish Reform," *Nineteenth Century*, XXIII (Feb., 1888), 276-296.

Faik Selânikli. "Die Geschichte der Freiheit und die Gedanken des Padischah; ein Beitrag zu den Entwickelungsphasen der Türkischen Freiheitsbewegung; nach dem in Konstantinopel 1324 (Finanzjahr=1326h=1908D) bei Karabet gedruckten Texte in Deutsche übersetzt von Theodor Menzel—Odessa," *Orientalisches Archiv*, I (Oct., 1910; Jan., 1911), 8-11; 60-69.

Fidel, Camille. "Le Comité Ottoman 'Union et Progrès,'" *Questions Diplomatiques et Coloniales*, XXVII (Apr., 1909), 438-446.

———— "L'Organisation de la Victoire Jeune-Turque: Le Comité 'Union et Progrès,'" *Questions Diplomatiques et Coloniales*, XXVII (June, 1909), 784-792.

Friedjung, Heinrich. "Die Türkische Revolution," *Die Woche*, X (Aug. 1, 1908), 1323-1325.

Fua, Albert. "Histoire du Comité Union et Progrès," *Mecheroutiette*, V (July, 1913), 37-45.

Gambier, James William. "The Life of Midhat Pasha," *Nineteenth Century*, II (Jan., 1878), 71-96.

———— "Macedonian Intrigues and their Fruits," *Fortnightly Review*, LXXVIII (Nov., 1902), 747-758.

Gates, C. Frank. "Turkey Under the New Régime," *Outlook*, XC (Nov., 1908), 531-533.

von der Goltz, Generalfeldmarschall C. Freiherr. "Die innerpolitische Umwälzung in der Türkei," *Deutsche Rundschau*, XXXV (Jan., 1909), 1-17.

———— "Die Politische Natur der heutigen Türkei," *Asiatisches Jahrbuch* (1912), 11-21.

Gottheil, Richard. "The Young Turks and Old Turkey," *Forum*, XL (Dec., 1908), 522-536.

Hachtmann, O. "Abdullah Dschewdet als Übersetzer," *Islamische Welt*, I (1917), 526-529.

———— "Die Neuere und Neueste Türkische Literatur: Eine Einleitung zu ihrem Studium," *Die Welt des Islams*, V (1917), 57-77.

———— "Türkische Übersetzungen aus Europäischen Literaturen: Ein Bibliographischer Versuch," *Die Welt des Islams*, VI (1918), 1-23.

Halid, Halil. "The Origin of the Revolt in Turkey," *Nineteenth Century*, LXV (1909), 755-760.

Hamilton, Angus. "Turkey: The Old Régime and the New," *Fortnightly Review*, XC (Sept., 1908), 369-382.

Hammer, S. C. "Den Tyrkiske Revolution," *Samtiden* (1909), 295-304.

Harrison, Frederic. "The Turkish Reform," *The Positivist Review*, XVII (Feb., 1909), 42-43.

Hartmann, Martin. "Abdulhamid," *Das Freie Wort*, IX (May, 1909), 121-130.

———— "Der Islam 1908," *Mitteilungen des Seminars für Orientalische Sprachen zu Berlin*, XII: 2. Abt. (1909), 33-108.

———— "Die neuere Literatur zum Türkischen Problem," *Zeitschrift für Politik*, III (1909), 159-189.

Herbert, Aubrey. "Talaat Pasha," *Blackwood's Magazine*, CCXIII (April, 1923), 425-440.

von Herbert, F. W. "Kamil Pasha and the Succession in Turkey," *Fortnightly Review*, XC (Sept., 1908), 419-429.

Huart, Cl., "Les Derviches Bektachis," *Revue du Monde Musulman*, IX (Oct., 1909), 235-246.

Hubka, Gustav. "Die Reformaktion in Makedonien in den Jahren 1320-1324 (1904-1908)," *Streffleurs Militärische Zeitschrift* (June, 1909), 913-926.

Imhoff, Generalmajor z. D. "Die Entstehung und der Zweck des Comites für Einheit und Fortschritt," *Die Welt des Islams*, I (1913), 167-177.

"L'Italia e la Nuova Turchia," *Nuova Antologia*, CXXXVII (Sept., 1908), 141-148.

BIBLIOGRAPHY

Izzet Fuad-Pascha, General. "Türkische Streiflichter aus der Aera Abd ul Hamid," *Deutsche Revue*, XXXVIII (Aug., 1913), 129-144.

Jacob, Georg. "Die Bektaschijje in ihrem Verhältnis zu verwandten Erscheinungen," *Abhandlungen der Philosophisch-Philologischen Klasse der Königlich Bayrischen Akademie der Wissenschaften*, XXIV: 3. Abt. (1909), 1-53.

Jäschke, Gotthard. "Die Entwicklung des osmanischen Verfassungsstaates von den Anfängen bis zur Gegenwart," *Die Welt des Islams*, V (1917), 5-56.

Jenkins, Hester Donaldson. "The Great Assassin," *Asia*, XVIII (April, 1918), 297-306.

Kızıldoğan, Hüsrev Sami. "Vatan ve Hürriyet=Ittihat ve Terakki [Fatherland and Liberty=Union and Progress]," *Belleten*, I (July-Oct., 1937), 619-625.

Kohn, Hans. "Der Arabische Nationalismus," *Zeitschrift für Politik*, XVII (1927), 26-46.

Krischtschian, Melkin. "Türken und Armenier in Vergangenheit und Gegenwart," *Der Orient*, XI: 2 & 3 (March-April & May-June, 1929), 37-46; 67-79.

Lang, Sir R. Hamilton. "The New Régime in Turkey," *Proceedings of the Central Asian Society*, XXVIII (1910).

LeChatelier, A. "Politique Ottoman," *Revue du Monde Musulman*, X (Jan., 1910), 93-103.

——— "Politique Musulmane: Lettre à un Conseiller d'État," *Revue du Monde Musulman*, XII (Sept., 1910), 1-165.

——— "Révolutions d'Orient," *Revue Politique et Littéraire: Revue Bleue*, 5th Series, X (Aug., 1908), 193-199.

Malleterre, Lieutenant-Colonel. "L'Armée Jeune-Turque," *Revue des Sciences Politiques*, XXVI (Sept., 1911), 734-755.

Marchand, H. "La Turquie et les Pays Arabes," *Questions Diplomatiques et Coloniales*, XXIX (May, 1910), 553-564.

——— "Réflexions sur la Crise Turque," *Questions Diplomatiques et Coloniales*, XXVII (May, 1909), 569-580.

Margoliouth, D. S. "Constantinople at the Declaration of the Constitution," *Fortnightly Review*, XC (Oct., 1908), 563-570.

Marillier, L. "La Maladie du Sultan," *Pro-Armenia*, I (10 April, 1901), 73-76.

[Midhat Bey, Ali Haydar]. "Die Aktion der Jungtürken: Eine Unterredung mit Ali Haydar Midhat Bey, Sohn Midhat Paschas," *Das Freie Wort*, VIII (Aug., 1908), 368-371.

Mülinen, Dr. E. Graf von. "Türken und Araber: Eine Historische Skizze," *Deutsche Revue*, XXXIII (Dec., 1908), 283-299.

Mundji Bey. "The New Constitution in Turkey," *The Independent*, LXV (Aug., 1908), 361-364.

——— "The Regenerated Ottoman Empire," *North American Review*, CLXXXVIII (Sept., 1908), 395-403.

"La Nuova Turchia," *Nuova Antologia*, CXXXVI (Aug., 1908), 652-662.

"L'Oeuvre de la 'Jeune Turquie.' Notes de Constantinople," *Études*, CXVIII (Jan., 1909), 119-235.

Pears, Edwin. "The Crisis in Turkey," *Contemporary Review*, XCV (May, 1909), 511-526.

——— "The Turkish Revolution," *Contemporary Review*, XCIV (Sept., 1908), 286-300.

Persignac, Comte Am. de. "Les Gaités de la Censure en Turquie," *La Revue*, LXVII (April, 1907), 384-393; 521-537.

Pfeiffer, Maximilian. "Abdul Hamid," *Südost*, V (Aug., 1918), 319-348.

Pinon, René. "La Turquie Nouvelle," *Revue des Deux Mondes*, 5th period, XLVII (Sept., 1908), 125-158.

"Pro-Islamite." "Turkish Revelations," *Westminster Review*, CLXXII (Aug., 1909), 117-129.

Riggs, C. T. "The New Era in Turkey," *Edinburgh Review*, CCVIII (Oct., 1908), 487-526.

Risal, P. "La Presse Turque," *La Revue*, LIX (Dec., 1905), 373-384.

Riza, Ahmet. See Ahmet Riza.

Rolfsen, Halvar B. "Brev fra Konstantinopel," *Samtiden* (1908), 581-586.

Rossier, Ed. "Trente-trois ans de règne; le Sultan Abdul-Hamid II," *Bibliothèque Universelle et Revue Suisse*, LIV (June, 1909), 570-601.

Rouire, Dr. "La Jeune-Turquie et l'avenir du Panislamisme," *Questions Diplomatiques et Coloniales*, XXVIII (Sept., 1909), 257-270.

Sakasow, Janko. "Die Türkische Revolution," *Sozialistische Monatshefte*, XIV (Aug., 1908), 1037-1040.

"The Secret of the Turkish Revolution," *The Spectator*, CI (Aug., 1908), 254-256.

S[lousch], N. "Les Deunmeh, une Secte Judéo-Musulmane de Salonique," *Revue du Monde Musulman*, VI (Nov., 1908), 483-495.

Slousch, N. "Le Nouveau Régime Turc et Tripoli," *Revue du Monde Musulman*, VI (Sept., 1908), 52-57.

Snouck Hurgronje, C. "Jong-Turkije; Herinneringen uit Stambol, 25 Juli-23 September 1908," *De Gids*, 4th series, XXVII (1909), 63-96.

Stavrianos, L. S. "The Balkan Committee," *Queen's Quarterly*, XLVIII (Autumn, 1941), 258-267.

Stead, Alfred. "Great Britain and Turkey; a Plea for a Sane Policy," *Fortnightly Review*, LXXXIX (March, 1908), 417-427.

"The Story of the Young Turks," *Blackwood's Magazine*, CLXXXV (Jan., 1909), 1-12.

Sussnitzki, Alphons J. "Das Postwesen in der Türkei," *Das Freie Wort*, VIII (Feb., 1909), 830-834.

Temperley, Harold. "Reform Movement in the Turkish Empire and Republic during the 19th and 20th Centuries," *Chinese Social and Political Science Review*, XX (1937), 449-460.

"Die Türkei vor den beiden letzten Kriegen 1910/1911; Auszüge aus den Aufzeichnungen und dem Tagebuch eines Diplomaten,"

Deutsche Revue, Jhrg. xxxviii: 2 & 3 (April-Sept., 1913), 43-53; 221-231; 298-312; 15-29; 202-212; 334-342.

"Die Türkische Armee," *Streffleurs Militärische Zeitschrift* (March, 1909), 487-504.

Vaka, Demetra. "An Imperial Enemy of Turkish Despotism; how the young Prince Sabaheddine outwitted the Spy of 'Abdul the Damned,' " *Asia*, xxiv (Jan., 1924), 32-36; 72-73.

——— "Prince Sabaheddine as a Free-Lance Liberal; how he broke with the Young Turks of Paris Boulevards and Cafés and of Official Stamboul," *Asia*, xxiv (Feb., 1924), 120-123; 150-151.

——— (Brown, Demetra Kenneth). "Women in the Young Turks Movement," *Atlantic Monthly*, ciii (May, 1909), 696-701.

la Valette St. George, Freiherr von. "Aus der Alten und Jungen Türkei," *Deutsche Revue*, xli:3 (July, Aug., 1916), 54-67; 225-233.

Vambéry, Arminius. "Europe and the Turkish Constitution," *Nineteenth Century*, lxiv (Aug., 1908), 224-229.

——— "Freiheitliche Bestrebungen im Moslimischen Asien," *Deutsche Rundschau*, xx (Oct., 1893), 63-75.

——— "The Future of Constitutional Turkey," *Nineteenth Century*, lxv (March, 1909), 361-374.

——— "Personal Recollections of Abdul Hamid and his Court," *Nineteenth Century*, lxv (June, 1909), 980-993; lxvi (July, 1909), 69-88.

"Viator." "The Turkish Revolution," *Fortnightly Review*, xc (Sept., 1908), 353-368.

Walther, Andreas. "Renaissance der Türkei," *Preussische Jahrbücher*, clxxiii (Aug., 1918), 158-170.

Winfrid, Ferdinand. "Armenier und Türken," *Preussische Jahrbücher*, clxxvi (June, 1919), 373-392.

Zander, Kurt. "Türkei; Rückblicke und Ausblicke," *Deutsche Revue*, xxxiv:4 (Oct., Nov., 1909), 26-33; 205-212.

Index